SOUTHWESTERN
SOUPS, STEWS, & SKILLET SUPPERS

by **JUDY WALKER** and **KIM MacEACHERN**

photography by
CHRISTOPHER MARCHETTI

NORTHLAND PUBLISHING

For our grandmothers,
Ruby Lee and Lucile,
Winnie and Kate—
you stood before us and
showed us the way.

— J. W.

—K. M.

The publisher wishes to thank Dillard's Department Store
in Flagstaff, Arizona, for their generous loan of props.

The text type was set in Adobe Garamond and Syntax
The display type was set in Pitchfork
Composed in the United States of America

Art Director: DAVID JENNEY
Designer: BILLIE JO BISHOP
Editor: BRAD MELTON
Book Editor: KATHLEEN BRYANT
Production Supervisor: LISA BROWNFIELD

Printed in Hong Kong by Wing King Tong Company Limited

All cooking temperatures in this book refer to the Fahrenheit scale.
The use of trade names does not imply an endorsement by the product manufacturer.

www.northlandpub.com

FIRST IMPRESSION
ISBN 0-87358-760-x

Walker, Judy Hille.
    Southwestern soups, stews, and skillet suppers / by Judy Walker and Kim
MacEachern.
        p.   cm.
    Includes index.
    ISBN 0-87358-760-X (alk. paper)
    1. Soups. 2. Casserole cookery. 3. Cookery, American–Southwestern style. I.
MacEachern, Kim. II. Title.

TX757 . W29 2000
641.8'2–dc21   00-035472

158/7.5M/8-00

COVER PHOTO: Skillet Enchiladas.
BACK COVER PHOTOS: Summer Gazpacho with Corn and Green Chiles, Eat-Your-
Veggies Chorizo Bake, and Fiesta Risotto.

CONTENTS

There is nothing more Southwestern than a pot of posole, nothing more Western than a chuckwagon beef stew. These one-pot dishes conjure up ancient images, such as the Native American stews of squash, chile, and beans, and not-so-ancient ones, such as the hearty chiles served to the hands on Kim's great-grandfather's cattle ranch in Liberty, Arizona.

But don't worry. We're not going to ply you with recipes for traditional Son of a Bitch Stew, as the cowboys called it, made from parts of the cow you don't even want to discuss. While we fully appreciate the influences of our region, we live, work, and write in the real world of forty-hour-plus workweeks, kids and family, endless obligations, and making time for friends. Most of the time, getting dinner on the table is a joy, but it's also a chore. And the thought of feeding guests can be overwhelming.

Thus was born this cookbook. It features manageable meals—mostly main dishes—not a lot of dishes to wash, and no ingredients that are going to break the bank. Many are interesting enough for a casual dinner party. We love to cook from scratch, but we also use convenience products. We give you some of our favorite basic meal-starters that you can make on the weekend and freeze for big flavor payoffs at a later date. But, hey. If you want to use canned chicken broth, that's fine.

That canned chicken broth—and frozen, should you choose to make it—should be part of every organized household. Our biggest resource is our pantry. Keep it stocked, keep your favorite things in it, and you'll never lack a quick meal solution. Here's what we keep in our Southwestern kitchens:

PANTRY LIST

We often keep the same ingredients on hand in numerous forms. For example: frozen chicken breasts and canned chicken, frozen roasted whole green chiles, and canned whole green chiles. This seeming duplication just increases our options. Out of canned broth? No problem, there's some in the freezer.

FRESH *Keep on Hand Most of the Time*

Onions: yellow, white, and red

Garlic

Limes

Lemons

Potatoes, new and bakers

Sweet potatoes

Winter squash, in season

REFRIGERATOR

Green onions

Cilantro, parsley

Cheeses: Cheddar (longhorn, sharp, white), Parmesan,
      Monterey jack, Mexican cheeses (see discussion
      that follows this list)

Carrots

Celery

Lemon juice (bottled)

Lime juice (bottled)

Catsup

Salsa

Cabbage

Eggs

Butter

Garlic, diced (bottled)

Sour cream

Dijon mustard

Mayonnaise

FREEZER

Chicken: Boneless, skinless breasts; thighs; wings; whole
      chickens

Ground beef or ground sirloin, ground pork, ground lamb

Chorizo

Stew meat

Pork roast

Shrimp

Chicken broth

Beef broth

Vegetable broth

Peas

French green beans

White corn

Corn tortillas

Cornmeal

Mango pieces

PACKAGED AND CANNED

Soups and Broth: Chicken, beef, and vegetable broth; Cheddar cheese soup; Fiesta Nacho soup; Tomato soup; onion soup mix; and condensed cream soups: Mushroom, chicken, celery

Oils: Olive, canola, vegetable

Corn

Tomatoes: Diced tomatoes, tomatoes with green chiles, tomato sauce, tomato paste, and sundried tomatoes

Beans, dried and canned: Pinto, Great Northern, heirloom beans, garbanzos, black-eyed peas, bean combination mixtures, black beans, small white beans, canned refried beans

Tuna

Green enchilada sauce

Red enchilada sauce

Salsa

V-8 juice

Jalapeños, canned and pickled

Chipotles in adobo sauce

Potato flakes

Garlic: Powdered, granulated, pickled

Minced dried onion flakes

Bay leaves

Chiles: Green chiles, whole and diced; jalepeños, canned and pickled; chipotles in adobo sauce; and dried chiles: All kinds (see Chiles discussion at end of this list)

Spices: Cayenne (red pepper); pure red chile powder; chili powder; red chile flakes; cumin, seeds and powdered; coriander, seeds and powdered

Pine nuts

Mexican pepitas or shelled pumpkin seeds

Rice: Basmati, Tex-Mati, arborio, brown, long grain

Pasta: Fideo, egg noodles, angel hair, spaghetti

Crackers

Croutons

Pasteurized processed cheese, with and without jalapeños

Tortillas: Flour, corn, chips

Nonstick cooking sprays: Plain, olive oil, butter flavor

Dried fruit: Prunes and apricots

Vinegars: Rice and seasoned rice, red wine, apple cider vinegar

Almonds

Tapioca

For convenience, we have classified the recipes according to an important aspect of the dish.

Look for this box: **Quick and Easy**

Though most are self-explanatory, a few may need elaboration:

Don't Miss: A special dish, one of our favorites.
Second Time Around: Use ingredients for more than one meal.
Quick and Easy: A snap to make.
Slow Cooker: Throw it all in your Crock-Pot.
Two Meals: Use this dish for more than one meal.
Family Favorite: Kids will love it!
Entertaining: Perfect for guests.
Traditional: Our variation on a classic dish.
Make Ahead: Keeps well, prepare in advance.

A Few Mexican-Style Cheeses

FRESH

Asadero: Mild, moist, slices easily, and melts well.
Panela: Mild, moist, resembles cottage cheese. Doesn't melt, but softens. Great with fruit and in salads.

SEMI-HARD

Cotija: Salty, pungent, semi-firm, crumbles easily. Resembles feta. Great over black beans and salads and as a contrast to sweeter dishes, such as whipped acorn squash.
Queso blanco: Mild, a little tangy, melts well. Great in fondues and cooked dishes and on sandwiches.

HARD

Queso anejo (aged cotija): Strong, aged flavor and dry texture. Good for shredding onto cooked dishes. Also good with salads and fruit.

Broth, Beans, and Chiles

With an understanding of the basic components of one-pot Southwestern cooking, you can complement your pantry list with these homemade ingredients and store them. You will be ready for anything, and the result will taste as though you have been cooking for days. Making these recipes from scratch is one way to enjoy these foods if you can't find them where you live! For example, we have a recipe for Easy Basic Chorizo, the Southwestern sausage, in case you have a hard time finding it in your region. (It's also great if you want to make a more healthful version!)

Seasoning mixes add extra oomph and make great gifts. The chapter winds up with a few simple but delicious recipes for extras that are great for rounding out your meals.

BROTH

For years, Judy felt like she made inadequate soup. Soup was the one thing she just couldn't get a handle on: It always seemed to lack something. Learning to make broth solved this problem.

Making great broth is much easier than you might think. All you need is something from which to extract flavor, and a half or whole day when you are going to be hanging around the house doing other things. You never stir broth in the making, so it's easy to ignore while you're otherwise occupied.

Start with a chicken. Wash it and put it in a pot with an onion you've peeled and cut into quarters, a few stalks of celery, especially the hearts (leaves and all); a carrot (scrubbed or peeled), and whole spices, such as peppercorns, a garlic clove or two, and some dried thyme.

Or start with pan-roasted beef short ribs, for extra flavor.

Though the flavor won't be as complex, you can also skip the roasting step and simply toss the ribs in the pot with the vegetables and spices.

Cover the chicken or beef with cold water and bring it to a boil, then turn the heat down to the lowest possible simmer. A slow bubble should break the surface occasionally. Let it go for an hour or two, until it starts to smell really good. If you want to reserve the chicken or meat for soup or something else, fish it out of the pot after an hour. Let it cool and remove it from the bones. You can put the bones back in the broth and cook it longer, if you want.

At this point you can skim the fat off the surface of the broth. Use a spoon to lightly skim off the foam, and discard it along with the fat. The refrigerator method of fat skimming discussed below is far less labor intensive.

When the broth has cooked as long as you want it to, you can strain it. If you don't have cheese-cloth or a fine sieve, wet a cotton kitchen towel and line a colander with it. Slowly pour the broth through this arrangement into a large container. It might take a while to percolate all the way through; some of the fat will remain in the cloth. That's fine. (Rinse the towel thoroughly before you wash it.)

The broth is ready to be transformed into soup. Or you can let it cool, then cover it before refrigerating or freezing. When you refrigerate it, all the fat will rise to the top and you can easily skim it off.

If you freeze the broth, be sure to leave at least half an inch of empty space at the top of the jar or container as you fill it. Liquid expands as it freezes. Broth is also easily frozen in plastic freezer bags.

Here's what broth looks like in a recipe format:

Best Beef Broth

In a large stockpot combine the ribs, onion, garlic, bay leaves, peppercorns, salt, and water to cover. Bring to a lively boil. Reduce heat to a very slow simmer. Skim foam occasionally.

Cook for 1 to 2 hours, or longer if desired. If you want to use the meat for soup or another dish, remove the meat and bones from the broth after one hour, or when tender. Or you may remove the meat from the bones and return it to the broth.

When broth has simmered as long as you wish, strain it through a fine-meshed sieve into a large container. Refrigerate, covered, until fat has congealed and can be lifted from the surface.

Optional: For deeper flavor, roast the ribs before making broth. Place ribs in a dish with 2 bay leaves, salt, pepper, and a sprinkle of garlic powder. Roast ribs until brown, 50 to 60 minutes at 425 degrees. If desired, add onion and 2 carrots, peeled and halved, for the last 20 minutes of roasting, so they also become very brown. Scrape all contents of roasting pan into a large, deep pot to make broth.

MAKES AT LEAST TWO QUARTS.

¾	pound short ribs
1	onion, halved
2	cloves garlic
2	bay leaves
5	black peppercorns
2	teaspoons salt

Consummate Chicken Broth

1	whole stewing chicken or broiler/fryer, washed, with neck and giblets
1	large onion, halved
2–3	stalks celery with leaves, cut into large pieces
2	carrots, peeled and quartered
2	whole cloves
2	cloves garlic (optional)
	Several black peppercorns

Combine all ingredients in a large, deep pot and add water to cover. Bring to a lively boil. Reduce heat to simmer. Do not stir at any time. Skim fat and foam from top, if desired.

If using chicken meat for soup or another dish, remove it after the first hour. Check to see if meat is done by cutting into thigh; if the meat is pink, keep cooking. When meat is done, let it cool enough to handle before removing from bones. Use broth as is or, if desired, return bones to broth and let simmer another hour or two to concentrate flavors.

When finished, strain broth through a fine-meshed sieve into a large container. Skim fat or, if you have time, cover bowl and refrigerate until fat has congealed on the surface and can be removed.

Use immediately or place in sealed containers and refrigerate up to 2 days or freeze for up to 6 months.

MAKES AT LEAST TWO QUARTS. A 3–4 POUND CHICKEN YIELDS 2 TO 4 CUPS COOKED MEAT.

Desert Seafood Broth

Fish heads and bones, the common basis for fish stock, are not as plentiful here in the desert as they might be elsewhere. We accumulate seafood shells in a bag in the freezer when we cook seafood chowder or grilled shrimp. When we have enough we make this stock, which is fat-free and keeps well in the freezer.

Combine all ingredients in a large, deep pot and bring to a rolling boil. Boil 10 minutes, then reduce heat and simmer for 1 hour.

Strain through a fine-meshed sieve. Use immediately or place in sealed containers and refrigerate up to 2 days or freeze up to 2 months.

MAKES ABOUT 6 CUPS.

1	large onion, quartered
2	stalks from the center of a bunch of celery, with leaves
	Shells from 3 lobster tails
	Peels from 1 pound shrimp
8	cups water
12	black peppercorns
3	white peppercorns
2	teaspoons dried thyme
4	teaspoons dried parsley
2	tablespoons lemon juice
4	whole cloves
1	teaspoon anchovy paste
½	cup dry sherry

Versatile Vegetable Broth

1	tablespoon oil
1	onion, chopped
1½	cups chopped root vegetables, such as carrot, parsnip, turnip, etc.
1	cup chopped celery, with leaves
	Other chopped vegetables as available, such as mushrooms, tomatoes, salad greens, etc., to taste
3	large sprigs fresh parsley
3	large sprigs fresh thyme, or 1 teaspoon dried
2	cloves garlic
1	bay leaf
3	whole cloves
6	whole black peppercorns
½	teaspoon salt
1	dried red chile (any size, any kind)
16	cups water and/or vegetable cooking liquid, as available

Making vegetable stock is a wonderful way to clean out your vegetable bin. Some of the stronger vegetables—such as broccoli, cauliflower, kale, or turnip greens—might overpower the broth, but you can use just about anything else, even salad greens that are in less-than-stellar shape. Chopping the vegetables roughly exposes more surface space to give up flavors. And if you're really ambitious, set aside a place in the freezer to save nutritious peelings—such as potato skins, tomato parings, the tops from green onions—or the water from cooking vegetables. Your stock will be different, but wonderful, every time you make it.

Heat oil in a large, deep pot. Add onion and sauté until browned. Add the rest of the ingredients. Bring to a boil. Reduce heat, cover loosely, and let simmer at least one hour. When vegetables have given up their flavor, strain broth into a large, deep pot to use immediately or into containers to refrigerate or freeze.

MAKES ABOUT 12 TO 14 CUPS, DEPENDING ON HOW LONG YOU LET IT SIMMER.

BASIC PINTO BEANS

A pot of pinto beans is a staple atop Southwestern stoves. Cooked beans make a soul-satisfying basic meal, and their broth can be used to add another dimension to your favorite soup or stew. Of course, the beans can be "refried" to make another basic building block of homestyle Southwestern food, great on the side or the main attraction in a burro. We use refried beans as a thickening agent in some recipes. Judy's son's first solid food was refried beans, and he still loves bean burritos.

To add that special picante dimension of Southwestern flavor, simmer your beans with a dried chile.

Use the following method to cook any number of dried beans: Great Northern beans for chilis, black beans, small white beans, or the heirloom varities such as Anasazi and bolitos, if you're lucky enough to find them.

To prepare beans for cooking, pick them over carefully, looking for stones. Wash in a colander.

Traditional soaking method: Place the beans in a large bowl. Cover the beans with water and let sit overnight.

Quick-soak method: Place the beans in a large, deep pot. Cover the beans with water one inch above the beans; bring to a boil for 2 minutes; cover the pan tightly with a lid and remove from heat. Let sit one hour.

Stove-top and slow-cooker methods: Drain the soaking water and in a large, deep pot cover beans with fresh water. Add optional ham (ends from a whole ham, ham hocks, or pieces of ham) if using. Bring to a boil, reduce to a simmer, and let cook for 2 hours. For a slow cooker, simply cook on high according to the manufacturer's instructions, usually 6 to 8 hours.

Pressure cooker method: Consult your manufacturer's instructions. Usually, you cover beans with water in the bottom of the cooker, being careful not to fill the cooker more than half full. Some directions say to use 2 cups water to each cup of beans, and to add 1 tablespoon oil to each cup of beans to help prevent foaming. If you have not soaked the beans, bring to a boil for 2 minutes. Cover with pressure cooker lid and remove from heat. Let cool for about 30 minutes. Remove lid; drain water. Add seasonings and as much fresh water as needed to meet the requirements of your pressure cooker. Replace the lid, bring up to pressure over high heat, and finish cooking according to manufacturer's instructions.

After cooking, remove any bones and skin from the ham, if used.

CHILES

Chiles are the soul of much Southwestern cooking. There is a bit of mystery surrounding them, even to the seasoned Southwesterner, given the difficulty with following the names of many chiles. Essentially, chiles are all of the capsicum family, which includes peppers as well. Capsicum refers to their heat, which is contained in the inner membranes of the chile itself and can be quite irritating if one does not take care to keep contact at a minimum. Full of vitamin C, chiles are not only an eating adventure but nutritional as well.

Chiles come from two basic groups: green and red. The red color is often a characteristic acquired by green chiles as they dry.

Fresh green chiles include the poblano and a number of varieties that are named for the area in which they are grown, usually in California and New Mexico; these include the California and the Hatch varieties. But the most common green chile of all is the Anaheim. It is longer and more slender than the others, a bit lighter green in color, and the mildest of the green chiles. Green chiles include the almost-mainstream jalapeños (when smoked they become chipotles), serranos, and gueros. Unless we specify otherwise, our references to green chiles are for the Anaheim, California, or New Mexico varieties.

The icons of the Southwest, red chiles are often found hanging in bunches like bananas, called *ristras*. These are the ripe, dried forms of the green chiles. They usually carry the name of their land, such as New Mexico or California, but the dried poblano is known as the ancho. Red chiles include such varieties as japonés, pequin, tepín, chiltepin, de arbol, cayenne, catarina, and cascabel, to name a few.

Heat seekers worship the hottest of the chiles, the habanero. No matter which chile you choose, it is wise to wear thin rubber gloves while handling them to keep the capsicum off your fingers.

BASIC GREEN CHILE

Green chile con carne, commonly referred to as green chile, is one of the most basic and versatile dishes to come out of the Southwest. Kim's Grandma Kate, a native Arizonan, had a favorite order in Mexican restaurants: a bowl of green chile and a fresh flour tortilla. We bow down before its humble majesty.

Green chile is stew at its most basic: beef, vegetables, and broth. In central and southern Arizona, the most common appearance made by green chile is in a "burro," the common term for burrito. (They're so big here that the diminutive "ito," meaning "little," doesn't apply!)

In New Mexico, almost everything you order in a restaurant is covered by either red or green chile. We prefer our slightly gringo-ized version. Burros are only the beginning for this complex, rich, beefy sauce. You could literally eat green chile for a week without repeating a dish. This is why it's wise to make a large batch of basic green chile and freeze it in portions for later use.

One secret to especially rich green chile is the cut of beef you use. If you plan to eat it Grandma Kate–style, a good cut of beef, such as a round roast, is recommended. However, the precut stew chunks offered in most meat cases is perfectly acceptable for burros and casseroles. You could also buy top round or London broil steaks, when they're on sale, and cube them for green chile (or any of our stew recipes, for that matter).

In the desert Southwest, where it seems we have no change of seasons, the aroma of roasting green chiles is a sure sign that it is finally fall. In eastern Arizona and New Mexico, chile season brings out the roasters. At roadsides, produce stands, and in front of supermarkets, the vendors set up portable, rotary grills, turn on the propane fire, and roast fresh green chiles to order while you wait. You can try a sample to see if they're hot or mild. Hatch chiles are in great demand, from Hatch, New Mexico, where the soil conditions are optimal. Cooks take roasted chiles home in large amounts and freeze enough to last a year.

While the rotary grills are fine, efficient contraptions, anyone can roast green chiles at home any time of year on a gas stove or outdoor grill or under the oven broiler. Simply crank up the flame and place a fresh green chile directly over it by either holding it with tongs or a long fork, or laying it on the grate. Turn frequently and continue to roast until the skin is charred and begins to crack open.

If broiler-roasting, be sure to watch carefully and turn the chiles quite frequently by pulling out the rack. (Never reach in and turn them—ouch!) The at-home process takes about twenty to thirty minutes, depending upon the flame and how close the chiles are to it.

Have a paper bag ready, and when the chiles are evenly charred, remove them to the bag. Fold to seal in the chiles and let them cool. At that point, the skins should slip right off.

Remove the stems and seeds and you're ready to cook the chiles. Although this is much more work than cracking open a can, the benefits are indescribable. The roasting creates a delicious smell during the process that makes it all worthwhile. And green chile lovers treasure the fresh-roasted flavor that just isn't captured in the can. Roasted green chiles are a valued culinary gift. Friends give friends green chiles!

Note: To freeze green chiles, package 1 to 3 whole, roasted chiles in a plastic freezer bag. Flatten to remove any air. Seal and lay flat in the freezer. Best if used within 3 months.

Green-Chile con Carne

Whole green chiles are best for this stew because you can control the size of the dice. They are readily available in cans in the Mexican-food aisle of the supermarket.

There are several approaches to making green chile. Our favorite is the pressure-cooker method. Not only is it quick, but the pressurized cooking seals in and blends the flavors. The resulting consistency is simply superb.

See recipes on pages 112, 116, and 117 for Green-Chile Casserole, Green-Chile Noodles, and Green-Chile Burros in a Pan.

1½	pounds lean beef or stew meat, cubed into bite-size pieces
1	large onion, coarsely chopped
8–10	whole green chiles, peeled, seeded, and coarsely chopped
8–10	cloves garlic, chopped
3	cups water
2	teaspoons salt
1	teaspoon freshly ground black pepper
1	tablespoon cornstarch
¼	cup cold water

Place all ingredients (except cornstarch and ¼ cup water) in pressure cooker according to manufacturer's directions. You may have to adjust the volume of water accordingly.

Bring to full pressure according to manufacturer's instructions and cook for 20 to 30 minutes.

Reduce pressure to safely remove the lid. After the lid is removed, bring contents of the cooker to a boil over high heat. Blend the cornstarch into the ¼ cup cold water in a small bowl or cup. Stir into boiling mixture and cook until thickened, about 3 to 5 minutes.

MAKES 5 CUPS.

Alternative slow-cooker method: Substitute 2 tablespoons flour for the cornstarch and add 1 (10-ounce) can of diced tomatoes. Place tomatoes, meat, onion, chiles, garlic, 3 cups water, salt, and pepper in the slow cooker. Turn on low and cook for 6 to 8 hours, the longer the better.

Turn the slow cooker to the high setting for about 10 minutes. Make a smooth paste of the 2 tablespoons flour and ¼ cup water. Slowly stir into the simmering beef mixture until incorporated. Continue to cook, on high, for about another 30 minutes.

MAKES ABOUT 6 CUPS.

Alternative stove-top method: Use 5 cups of water instead of 3. Place ingredients (except cornstarch and ¼ cup water) in a large, deep pot. Cover and bring to a boil. Reduce the heat and simmer, partially covered (with the lid cocked on top of the pot to allow some steam to escape) for at least 2 hours, or until the meat is fork-tender. Return to boiling. Blend the cornstarch into the cold water in a small cup. Stir into the boiling beef mixture and cook until thickened.

MAKES ABOUT 5 CUPS.

Note: To freeze green chile con carne, package in rigid plastic containers with ½ inch of space on top or in gallon-size plastic freezer bags. Flatten bags to remove air. Seal and lay flat in the freezer. Best if used within six months.

Green-Chile Enchilada Sauce

You will think of dozens of ways to use this green chile enchilada sauce, and you will find several recipes in here that use it, such as Green Enchilada Sauce Chicken and Mashed Potatoes (page 97). Chicken is especially good cooked in or served under this sauce. We also really like it combined with Monterey jack or any of the tangy Mexican cheeses, such as asadero.

Heat oil in a saucepan over medium heat and sauté onion and garlic for 5 minutes. Stir in cornstarch to make a paste or roux and cook until the mixture begins to brown. Whisk in the broth, little by little, and bring to a simmer for a few minutes. Add coriander, oregano, cumin, and pepper after the first couple of broth additions. After broth has simmered, stir in green chiles. Taste and adjust seasoning, adding salt if needed.

MAKES ABOUT 4 CUPS.

2	tablespoons olive oil
½	large onion, chopped
2	cloves garlic, minced
3	tablespoons cornstarch
4	cups vegetable broth
½	teaspoon ground coriander
½	teaspoon dried oregano
½	teaspoon powdered cumin
½	teaspoon freshly ground black pepper
10	green chiles, chopped, roasted, peeled, and seeded (or used canned whole green chiles)
	Salt to taste

BASIC RED CHILE

Those strings of red chiles you see hanging all over Southwestern venues are not merely decoration (except, of course, the ceramic ones). The dried chiles on these ristras are the basis for staple sauces. Pork is commonly found stewing in red chile sauce. Enchiladas of all kinds are made with the red chile sauce. And the classic cross-dressing dish of the Southwest is the green chile burro, enchilada style—green chile inside, sauced with red!

Leaving your red chiles to hang is a perfect storage method. Just dust and wash them well before use. Rejuvenate chiles by soaking them in a bit of boiling water. The tricky part is using the right chile for the desired heat. Pure New Mexico red chile is the best, and it comes in milder or hotter variations. You can use the dried chiles themselves, or start with powdered red chile. But beware the "chili powder" that is found among the grocery store spices, because it contains a number of ingredients besides just the powdered chiles. Be sure to read the label!

As with green chile, there are several options for making enchilada sauce. We offer our favorites here. See recipes on pages 88 and 97 for several types of enchiladas, red and green.

Enchilada Sauce from Dried Chiles

Seed and stem the dried chiles. Heat a skillet over medium-high heat and lay the chiles flat to toast, turning often to avoid scorching. This process only takes a couple of minutes and greatly enhances the flavor. Transfer the chiles to a bowl, cover with the 2 cups of boiling water, and set aside for about 15 minutes. Transfer the chiles and about half of the soaking water to a blender or food processor and purée. Reserve the remaining water.

In a saucepan, heat the oil over medium heat and add flour, cumin, oregano, and coriander. Stir into a paste or roux and heat until bubbling, stirring for 2 or 3 minutes, until it begins to brown. Stir in the reserved soaking water from the chiles, a little at a time. Stir in garlic and honey and simmer until garlic is cooked. Add puréed chiles. At this point the mixture is still quite thick, so rinse the blender or food processor with the 1½ cups of water and whisk that into the pan, little by little. Stir in salt. Bring to a very gentle simmer (be patient!) for 20 minutes, stirring often. Adjust salt to taste.

MAKES 3 CUPS.

8–10	dried New Mexico red chiles
2	cups boiling water
1	tablespoon olive oil
1	tablespoon flour
½	teaspoon cumin
½	teaspoon dried oregano, crushed
½	teaspoon ground coriander
3	cloves garlic, minced
1	teaspoon honey
1½	cups water
½	teaspoon salt

2	tablespoons olive oil
4	tablespoons finely chopped onion
1	clove garlic, minced
½	teaspoon powdered oregano
1	teaspoon powdered cumin
2	tablespoons flour
½	cup powdered pure red chile
2½	cups water
2	ablespoons red wine vinegar
1	teaspoon salt

Enchilada Sauce from Red Chile Powder

Heat oil in a saucepan over medium heat. Add onion and garlic and sauté until golden. Add oregano, cumin, and flour. Stir to form a paste or roux and cook until it begins to brown. Add powdered red chile and stir to combine. Whisk in water and red wine vinegar, little by little, and bring gently to a simmer for about 5 minutes. Add salt.

MAKES 2½ CUPS.

Enchilada Sauce from Red Enchilada Mix

¼	cup olive oil
½	cup flour
1	cup Red Enchilada Mix (recipe follows)
4	cups water
¼	cup cider vinegar

This is the easiest and, we think, the tastiest method. It makes enough for a large pan of enchiladas. The red enchilada mix recipe can be doubled or tripled and stored in the freezer for spur-of-the-moment enchilada sauce. All you add is oil, flour, water, and vinegar.

Heat a saucepan over medium-high heat and add olive oil and flour. Stir to form a paste or roux. Continue to cook until mixture just begins to brown. Add seasoning mix and stir to combine. Slowly whisk in water, incorporating each addition to make a smooth, gravy-like consistency, over medium-high heat. Stir in vinegar. Bring to a gentle simmer, stirring continuously and cook for 10 minutes.

MAKES 5 CUPS.

Note: To freeze any enchilada sauce, package in rigid plastic containers with ½ inch space on top or in plastic freezer bags. Flatten bag to remove air. Seal and lay flat in freezer. Best if used within 3 months.

Red Enchilada Mix

Place all ingredients in a medium glass bowl. Use a wire whisk to evenly combine them. Store in an airtight container in the freezer.

MAKES 1 CUP.

¾	cup powdered pure red chile
1	tablespoon powdered coriander
1	tablespoon powdered cumin
1	tablespoon powdered oregano
1	tablespoon powdered garlic
1	tablespoon onion powder

SEASONING MIXES AND EXTRAS

Taco Seasoning Mix

¼ cup dried onion flakes

4 teaspoons cornstarch

4 tablespoons pure powdered red chile (not chili powder with other added ingredients)

3 teaspoons ground cumin

3 teaspoons garlic powder

2 teaspoons dried hot red pepper flakes

1½ teaspoons dried Mexican oregano

2 tablespoons salt

This is sugar-free, unlike the commercial versions. Try it in the recipe for Sloppy Josés on page 85.

Combine all ingredients well. Store airtight.

To make taco meat: Combine 3 tablespoons seasoning mix with ¼ cup water and add to 1 pound ground meat. Cook for 15 minutes, adding more water if needed.

MAKES ABOUT ½ CUP.

Southwest Seasoning Mix

1 tablespoon powdered cumin

1 tablespoon powdered oregano

1 ablespoon garlic powder

An all-around blend to keep on hand in a shaker to perk up soups, stews, salsa, salad dressings, stuffings, and chicken dishes.

Mix ingredients in a small container.

MAKES 3 TABLESPOONS. (TRIPLE RECIPE TO MAKE ABOUT 1 CUP.)

Basic Easy Chorizo

The chile-laden sausage of the Southwest is SOOO much better if you make it at home (or buy it from a reputable butcher). It is best when made ahead at least a few hours so the red chile powder can meld with the meat. Our chorizo recipe has many influences and includes tequila, which is a good substitute for the white vinegar found in most versions.

Combine all ingredients in a large bowl. Use your hands to mix well. Meat should be uniformly colored. You may use the chorizo mixture at once but, ideally, let flavors meld by covering it and letting it sit for a few hours in the refrigerator. It may also be frozen until ready for use.

MAKES 2 POUNDS.

1	pound lean ground beef
1	pound ground pork
4	tablespoons pure New Mexico red chile powder
¼	teaspoon pepper
½	teaspoon salt
1	teaspoon ground cumin
3	cloves garlic, crushed
3	tablespoons tequila

Basic Perfect Pie Pastry

3   cups flour

1   teaspoon salt

½   cup shortening

½   cup butter, softened

1   egg

5   tablespoons very cold water

1   teaspoon rice vinegar

    Nonstick cooking spray

Many pie pastry recipes call for vinegar. We recommend rice vinegar and, for a savory pie, seasoned rice vinegar. Kim's daughter, Melanie, loves to handle dough and she does a fine job of "cutting" the shortening or butter into the flour with a fork and knife, scraping the fork clean occasionally with the knife. A pastry blender makes the job even easier.

Try this with the Green-Chile Quiche on page 115.

In a large bowl, combine flour and salt. Cut in shortening and butter until the mixture has the consistency of cornmeal. In a separate bowl, beat together the egg, water, and vinegar. Sprinkle the liquid ingredients over the flour mixture and stir to combine, until it can be formed into a ball. On a flat surface coated with nonstick cooking spray, roll out the pastry until it is 3 inches larger than the diameter of the bottom of the pie pan or skillet.

MAKES ENOUGH FOR ONE LARGE PIE, SUCH AS THE BOTTOM CRUST OF THE GREEN CHILE QUICHE.

Croutons

You can use Southwest Seasoning Mix to sprinkle on these easy croutons. Use them in soups or salads. They are great when served warm.

Cube the bread and brush (or spray) with olive oil. Sprinkle with basil, cilantro, or seasoning mix. Dry in the toaster or conventional oven at 350 degrees for about 10 minutes, until lightly toasted.

MAKES ABOUT 2 CUPS.

3   slices French bread

Olive oil

Fresh basil or cilantro, chopped, or Southwest Seasoning Mix (page 25)

Southwest Garlic Toast

Garlic toast is a grown-up crouton, served on the side instead of in the soup. Does it get any easier or better than this?

Preheat oven to broil or 550 degrees. Cut bread into ½-inch slices and lay them on a cookie sheet. Spread each slice with butter, and sprinkle with seasoning mix or garlic salt and cheese. Place under the broiler. Watch carefully and remove when the cheese begins to bubble and brown.

MAKES ABOUT 8 SERVINGS.

1   loaf French bread (day-old bread works here)

1   stick butter, softened

Southwest Seasoning Mix (page 21) or garlic salt

½   cup freshly grated Parmesan cheese

Jalapeño Blue-Corn Muffins

We've been making these so long we have no idea where the recipe originally came from! Of course, if you can't find blue cornmeal in your area, you can substitute yellow or white meal.

Preheat oven to 400 degrees. Grease a 12-muffin tin or line it with cupcake papers. In a medium bowl sift together cornmeal, flour, baking powder, salt, and sugar. Add eggs and milk and beat until thoroughly blended. Stir in melted butter, cream, and peppers.

    Divide the batter evenly in the tin. Bake 15 minutes, until an inserted toothpick comes out clean and tops are lightly browned.

MAKES 12 MUFFINS.

1½	cups blue cornmeal
½	cup flour
1	ablespoon baking powder
1	teaspoon salt
1	teaspoon sugar
3	eggs, lightly beaten
1	cup milk
⅓	cup melted butter
¼	cup cream
⅓	cup seeded and finely diced jalapeño peppers
⅓	cup finely diced red bell pepper

LEFT: Jalapeño Blue-Corn Muffins and Instant Black-Bean Salad.

Real Salsa

1	(15-ounce) can diced tomatoes, or 2 large ripe tomatoes, chopped
1	(4-ounce) can chopped green chiles, or 3 roasted and peeled green chiles, diced
1	large onion, diced
1	jalapeño, finely minced (optional)
½	teaspoon oregano (optional)
¼	teaspoon ground cumin
1	tablespoon olive oil (optional)
	Salt and pepper

Salsa is a no-brainer with chips, but we also use it to jazz up soup and as a recipe ingredient, too. It's also great as a garnish.

Combine all ingredients in a medium bowl; season with salt and pepper to taste.

MAKES ABOUT 2 CUPS.

Black-Bean Salsa

This is quick, delicious, and nutritious. Try it as a garnish on White Chili (page 61).

Combine all ingredients and season with salt and pepper to taste. Chill.

MAKES ABOUT 2 ½ CUPS.

1	(15-ounce) can black beans, drained
2	tablespoons chopped red onion
¾	cup chopped tomato
	Juice of 1 lime
1	tablespoon chopped green chiles
1	teaspoon sugar
	Salt and pepper

Roasted Pepper Relish

This dip makes a nice spread for bread as is, or you may mix it with sour cream. Quantities can be cut in half to use the dip as a soup garnish.

In a food processor, finely chop the red and jalapeño peppers, olives, parsley, and garlic. Add sugar, olive oil, lemon juice, and salt and pepper to taste. Process just until mixed.

MAKES ABOUT 2 CUPS.

1	(14-ounce) jar roasted red peppers, or 3 large red bell peppers, roasted, peeled, and seeded
3	fresh jalapeño peppers, seeded
12	small green olives with pimentos
2	tablespoons chopped fresh parsley
1	teaspoon minced garlic
½	teaspoon sugar
4	teaspoons olive oil
1	tablespoon fresh lemon juice
	Salt and freshly ground black pepper

Instant Black-Bean Salad

1   (15-ounce) can black beans,
        drained and gently rinsed
1   tomato, chopped
½   large onion, chopped
     Juice of 1 lime
     Salt and freshly ground black
        pepper

Optional additions:
1   cup corn (canned, cooked, or
        frozen)
2–3 tablespoons chopped cilantro
2–3 tablespoons chopped green
        chiles, or 1 chopped jalapeño
1   clove garlic, minced
1   tablespoon olive oil

This is an incredibly versatile recipe, as you can tell from the list of optional additions! You can make it different every time.

Combine all ingredients in a medium bowl, seasoning to taste with salt and pepper.

MAKES 2 ½ CUPS (WITHOUT ANY OPTIONAL ADDITIONS).

Cilantro Pesto

Use this as a change of pace from basil pesto. Add to soup or toss with hot pasta for a simple side dish.

In a food processor, blend all ingredients except olive oil. While processor is running, slowly add olive oil in a steady stream. Cover and refrigerate. Keeps 2 to 3 days.

MAKES ABOUT ½ CUP.

1	cup packed cilantro leaves
2	teaspoons pine nuts
1½	teaspoons lime jiuce
1½	teaspoons minced garlic
1	tablespoon grated Parmesan cheese
	Salt and freshly ground black pepper
¼	cup olive oil

Avocado Dressing

Great on a simple green salad!

Combine ingredients in blender, adding salt to taste. Serve over lettuce or sliced tomato.

MAKES 1 CUP.

1	avocado, peeled
½	cup orange juice
1	tablespoon lemon juice
2	teaspoons mayonnaise
	Salt

31

Greens in Beer

2½	bunches cleaned mustard greens or turnip greens, torn into small pieces
1	(12-ounce) bottle of beer or ale
1	large onion, chopped
2	large cloves garlic, chopped
1	ham hock, or 4 to 6 ounces smoked pork butt (optional)
2	tablespoons molasses

At the Gospel Brunch at the House of Blues in Mandalay Bay resort in Las Vegas, Judy found sweet inspiration in the greens cooked in Dixie Beer. You can make these in the slow cooker and serve them on the side with any of the stews, beans, and meat dishes.

Pack the greens into a large (5-quart) slow cooker and pour beer over them. Cover and cook on the low setting for about 1 hour. Stir well and add remaining ingredients, stirring to combine. If the mixture seems dry, add ½ to 1 cup of water. Replace the cover and continue to cook on low 4 to 6 more hours.

If you use the ham, remove it from the slow cooker, chop, and return to the greens before serving.

MAKES 6 TO 8 SERVINGS.

SOUPS

Soup is basic, the liquid of life. Soup is found in literature, poetry, history, anthropology, and folklore. Soup is part of every culture, including the native Southwestern cultures. You can find it in the most luxurious restaurants and in soup kitchens, at once hedonism and sustenance. To us, soup symbolizes the simmering pot of global society. And best of all, soup is good for you, too.

Soup can be a recipe for improving the quality of life in our fast-paced, health-conscious, calorie-counting era of gastronomic contradictions. With the wider availability of Southwestern ingredients and the unavailability of time to experiment with them, this chapter is a road map to taking full advantage of these victuals with the minimum investment of time and money.

For almost two years, we traded soup. Each week, one of us made enough soup to feed both our families. Here's how it works if you want to find a dedicated pal. Starting with a recipe from this chapter, cook the soup. When completed, put half of it in a jar. Let it cool, seal with the lid and refrigerate. When you see your friend, pass along the soup jar. In the meantime, you will enjoy your reserved soup for a meal or two. Then just sit back and wait until you see your friend again next week. You will get the jar returned to you filled with another soup—another great meal or two, and with no cooking.

Almost all the following recipes came from our love affair with soup.

Sausage, Potato, and Green-Chile Soup

12	ounces reduced-fat bulk sausage
1	large onion, chopped
1	(4-ounce) can of chopped green chiles, or 4 green chiles, roasted, peeled, seeded, and chopped
2	cloves garlic, minced
2½	pounds potatoes, peeled and diced
4	cups chicken broth
4	(12-ounce) cans evaporated skim milk (6 cups)
1	teaspoon savory
	Freshly ground pepper

Potatoes and green chiles have a flavor affinity that's been exploited for as long as the two have been available in the Southwest. (A common breakfast item is the chorizo and potato burrito, with just enough green chile to keep it interesting.) This soup gets extra zip from bulk sausage; use the sage-flavored variety if you can find it.

In a large, deep pot, brown the sausage, breaking it into chunks as it cooks. Add onion and cook until translucent. Drain any drippings. Return sausage and onion to pot. Add green chiles, garlic, potatoes, and chicken broth. Bring to a boil, reduce heat, and simmer 20 to 25 minutes, until potatoes are tender. Add milk, savory, and pepper to taste. Heat over lowest heat until soup is hot. Serve.

MAKES 8 TO 10 SERVINGS.

Pinto-Bean and Fideo Soup

Fideo is a very thin Mexican pasta used in sopa seca, *or dry soup. This contradictory notion usually translates on the plate into semi-soupy noodles. Fideo (pronounced fuh-DAY-oh) is available in supermarkets that carry a good stock of Mexican ingredients, or you can use broken-up vermicelli or angel hair pasta. Here we combine fideo with pinto beans, which you may make the day before or use from a can. For a less picante-esque soup, substitute a jalapeño or a green chile (seeds and white membrane removed) for the chipotle.*

Place tomatoes, onion, garlic, and chipotle pepper in a food processor or blender (if using a blender, roughly chop the tomatoes, onion, and garlic first). Purée until smooth.

    Heat oil in a large, deep pot. Add fideo or angel hair pasta, stirring frequently to toast. Add pinto beans and tomato purée. Continue to cook over medium heat for 5 minutes. Add water and stir to combine. Cook for another 5 minutes.

MAKES 8 TO 10 SERVINGS.

Second Time Around

2	medium ripe tomatoes
1	medium onion
3	cloves garlic
1	chipotle pepper, canned in adobo sauce
2	tablespoons oil
7	ounces fideo or angel hair pasta broken into 2-inch lengths
6	cups cooked pinto beans and their broth (see recipe on page 12), or 4 (15-ounce) cans pinto beans, undrained
4	cups water

Tortilla Soup

6   cups chicken broth

1   cup red enchilada sauce,
        homemade (recipe on
        page 20) or canned

1   (10¾-ounce) can of condensed
        tomato soup

2   bay leaves

    Salt and freshly ground pepper

6–8 corn tortillas, cut into strips and
        fried until crisp

1   cup shredded cheese

Options:

    Chopped green onions

    Cooked beans (black or pinto)

    Chopped cilantro

    Lime juice

    Cooked ground beef or diced
        chicken or turkey

We had a wonderful Tortilla Soup recipe years ago and misplaced it. This one is "rebuilt" from our recollection and serves up in no time. To change the heat level, adjust the ratio of tomato soup to enchilada sauce. If you like it really spicy, use 2 cups enchilada sauce and omit the tomato soup altogether.

In a large, deep pot, combine broth, enchilada sauce, tomato soup, and bay leaves. Add salt and pepper to taste. Heat to a simmer and cook for 20 minutes. Remove bay leaves. Place chips in the bottom of large soup bowls. Sprinkle on cheese and any of the options you may desire. Cover with hot soup. Serve immediately.

MAKES 6 SERVINGS.

Quick and Easy

Black-Bean Soup with Sautéed Vegetables

This easy slow-cooker soup is finished quickly with an addition of sautéed vegetables.

Place soaked black beans in the slow cooker with a ham bone. Cover with several inches of fresh water. Cook on high for 6 to 8 hours.

   Heat the oil in a skillet and sauté the onion and garlic for 2 minutes. Add the green chiles and cook for 1 minute. Add the tomatoes and oregano and continue to cook until the tomato juice reduces. Stir the sautéed vegetables into the bean soup in the slow cooker.

   Ladle into bowls and garnish with a spoonful of sour cream.

MAKES 8 SERVINGS.

1	cup dried black beans (cleaned and soaked according to directions on page 11)
1	small ham bone, or 1 pound ham hocks (smoked or fresh)

To finish the soup:

1	tablespoon oil
½	cup chopped red onion
2	cloves garlic, minced
3	large roasted green chiles, peeled, seeded, and diced
1	(12-ounce) can stewed tomatoes
2	tablespoons stemmed and chopped fresh oregano, or 2 teaspoons dried
	Sour cream for garnish

1 pound lean ground sirloin

2 cloves garlic, minced

1 medium onion, chopped

3 stalks celery, chopped

3 carrots, chopped

½ cup flour

3 (14½-ounce) cans beef stock

2 medium potatoes, peeled
and diced

1½ teaspoons Worcestershire Sauce

1½ teaspoons Kitchen Bouquet

½ teaspoon salt

½ teaspoon pepper

Steak Soup

This hearty wonder came to us via Jean Scott, who used to be a chef for country clubs in Oklahoma and other states. We cut down the recipe, but you might want to double it for a special tailgating party!

In a large, deep pot, brown the beef. Add garlic and onion and cook 1 minute. Add celery and carrots; cook until tender. Add flour and stir to coat the beef and vegetables. Add stock, stirring to incorporate the flour. Add potatoes and simmer 5 minutes. Add Worcestershire sauce, Kitchen Bouquet, salt, and pepper and continue to simmer 10 to 15 minutes, or until potatoes are tender.

MAKES 6 SERVINGS.   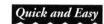 *Quick and Easy*

---

1 onion, coarsely chopped

1 pound flank steak, cut into
1-inch squares

3 cloves garlic, minced

4 green chiles, roasted and coarsely
chopped, or 1 (4-ounce) can
chopped green chiles

Flank Steak Soup, Phoenix Style

We have always loved to grill the flank steak stuffed with green chiles and cheese from the Phoenix Market, a long-time neighborhood butcher shop. Later, we discovered that the Phoenix City Grille stuffs steaks with green chiles and cheese, allowing you to order your New York strip "Phoenix style."

Of course, that instantly became a favorite as well. Here we have expanded the concept to make a delightful soup.

In a slow cooker, combine the onion, steak, garlic, chiles, salt, and water. Stir in the soup. Cook for 6 to 8 hours on low or 4 hours on high. During the last hour, add the beer.

Serve topped with shredded Cheddar cheese.

MAKES 4 TO 6 SERVINGS.

1	teaspoon salt
3	cups water
1	(10¾-ounce) can condensed Cheddar cheese soup
1	(12-ounce) bottle beer
2	cups shredded Cheddar cheese

Many-Bean Soup

A favorite soup around Kim's house turned into a craft one holiday season when she had too much time on her hands and started hot-gluing the beautiful uncooked beans to form a topiary tree. In the process she learned that this particular package of bean mix, labeled "15 bean soup," had only 13 kinds of beans! The mix is also available in the 17-bean variety (which we haven't examined closely for truth in advertising).

Place beans, water, onion, garlic, and herbs in the slow cooker and cook on low for 6 to 8 hours. Add tomatoes and the lemon juice and let cook long enough to heat through.

MAKES 10 TO 12 LARGE SERVINGS.

1	(1-pound) package of 13–, 15–, or 17–bean mix, soaked and drained
8	cups water
1	onion, coarsely chopped
3	cloves garlic, peeled
1	bay leaf
1	teaspoon dried oregano
1	(14½-ounce) can peeled tomatoes
	Juice of 1 lemon

39

Summer Gazpacho with Corn and Green Chiles

4	large, very ripe tomatoes, diced
2	cucumbers, finely diced
2	stalks celery, finely diced
3	green onions, finely diced
4	cloves garlic, minced
1	(64-ounce) can tomato-vegetable cocktail or vegetable juice (8 cups)
1	cup canned (drained) or frozen corn, thawed
2	tablespoons diced green chiles
½	teaspoon hot pepper sauce, or more to taste
	Salt and freshly ground black pepper
	Croutons for garnish

When it's just too darned hot to cook in the summer, grab a can of V-8 Juice and use it as the base for this refreshing gazpacho variation. Homemade croutons are a crispy compliment to this cooling soup (see recipe on page 25).

Mix tomatoes, cucumbers, celery, onions, and garlic in a large bowl. Stir in juice, corn, chiles, and hot pepper sauce. Season with salt and pepper to taste.

   Garnish with croutons before serving. Keeps in refrigerator for several days.

MAKES 6 TO 8 SERVINGS.

OPPOSITE: Many-Bean Soup and Summer Gazpacho with Corn and Green Chiles.

The King's Courtship Peanut Butter Soup

1	chicken (4 to 5 pounds), cut up
2	tablespoons peanut oil
2	medium onions, chopped
2	teaspoons chopped garlic
¾	cup chunky peanut butter
¼–½	teaspoon cayenne, or to taste
½	teaspoon salt
	Pepper
1	bunch spinach, washed and coarsely shredded
½	cup roasted, salted peanuts, chopped

In 1997, when Sule Issifu lived in Queen Creek, Arizona, he was called home to his duty, to be the king of the Mamprusi tribe of Ghana, West Africa, upon the death of his father, the reigning king. Our dear friend, Barbara Yost, was lucky enough to join the new King and his family for dinner just before they made their journey back to his 250,000 subjects. He served this traditional West African soup, which stole his wife Lydia's heart during their dating days in Oregon. Although his exact recipe is a royal family secret, Barbara assures us this is a fine replica. Because it uses cayenne, and because we thought you would love this soup's story as much as we do, we have decided it qualifies as Southwestern.

Step One (may be done up to one day in advance): In a large, deep pot, cover chicken with water and bring to a boil. Cover the pot, reduce the heat, and simmer until the chicken is just done, about an hour. Remove the chicken and reserve broth. Cool chicken pieces; remove skin and shred chicken. Refrigerate chicken and broth unless using within 30 minutes.

Step Two: In a large, deep pot, heat oil and sauté onions and garlic for 3 minutes. Add shredded chicken and broth. Heat to a boil and reduce to a simmer. Remove about a cup of hot broth and mix with the peanut butter, adding more as needed to form a smooth paste. Add the peanut butter mixture to the soup, along

with cayenne, salt, and pepper to taste. Add spinach and cook 5 minutes. Add chopped peanuts. Stir and serve to someone you love.

Option: Rather than shredding the chicken, use whole, skinless pieces in the soup.

MAKES 8 SERVINGS.    *Family Favorite*

Chicken, Corn, and Green-Chile Chowder

To make this easy chowder into a vegetarian entrée, omit the chicken and use water or vegetable broth. (Of course, you'll skip the bacon bits, too!)

In a large, deep pot, heat oil and add onion and chicken. Cook until brown. Add bell pepper and chiles and continue to cook, stirring frequently, until the vegetables are tender. Add broth and heat just to boiling. Add corn and lower heat. Season to taste with garlic powder and pepper. Add milk. Heat through but do not boil. Serve topped with bacon bits.

MAKES 8 TO 10 SERVINGS.    *Family Favorite*

2	tablespoons oil
1	large onion, chopped
3	boneless, skinless chicken breasts, diced
1	red bell pepper, chopped
2	green chiles, roasted, peeled, and diced, or 1 (4-ounce) can chopped green chiles
6	cups chicken broth
1	pound frozen white corn (or yellow if you can't find the white)
	Garlic powder
	Freshly ground black pepper
2	quarts low-fat milk, evaporated skim milk, or half-and-half
	Bacon bits

Calabacitas Soup

If you're lucky, you'll find calabacitas as a side dish in Mexican restaurants. We love this squash and vegetable combination so much that Judy just had to make it into soup!

Heat oil in a large, deep pot and sauté onion, bell pepper, and garlic. When aromatic, add tomatoes, squash, and broth. Stir well and cook 10 minutes. Add corn and chicken. Cook another 5 minutes. Serve topped with cheese.

MAKES 6 TO 8 SERVINGS.  *Quick and Easy*

1	tablespoon oil
1	large onion, chopped
1	green bell pepper, chopped, or 2 tablespoons chopped green chile
1	red bell pepper, chopped
2	cloves garlic, chopped
1	fresh tomato, chopped, or 1 (12-ounce) can diced tomatoes
2	crookneck or yellow squash, chopped
2	medium zucchini squash, sliced
8	cups chicken broth
1	(11-ounce) can whole kernel corn, undrained
2	cups cooked chicken, diced
1	cup Cheddar cheese, shredded

LEFT: Christmas Posole and Calabacitas Soup.

Our Easy Posole

1   tablespoon olive oil

½   onion, chopped

½   teaspoon minced garlic

1   (4-ounce) can chopped green
        chiles

1   (29-ounce) can yellow or white
        hominy, with liquid

1   (14½-ounce can stewed tomatoes

1   (14½-ounce can beef broth or 2
        cups water

½   teaspoon ground cumin

½   teaspoon dried oregano

1   cup cooked chicken or pork

        Garnish with any or all: lime or
           lemon wedges, sliced
           radishes, chopped cilantro,
           red pepper flakes, dried
           Mexican oregano

Posole is a cold-weather Southwestern tradition. Judy has been excited about posole since the first time she ate it years ago at an Arizona Republic *holiday potluck lunch, where it was prepared with lots of red chili powder by the late Carle Hodge, the newspaper's science writer.*

For a special occasion, serve with lots of garnishes. Remember this recipe, too, when you have leftover chicken, turkey, or pork.

In a large, deep pot, heat olive oil and add onions and garlic. Sauté until the onions begin to wilt. Add green chiles and stir 1 or 2 minutes longer. Add remaining ingredients and stir. Bring to a boil, reduce heat, and simmer for 20 minutes.

Serve with garnishes, if desired.

MAKES 6 SERVINGS.

Joyce's Albóndigas Soup

We are not sure who Joyce is, but we know for sure that this recipe has been an Arizona favorite for years. Albóndigas soup always has meatballs. In restaurants they range from tiny to half the size of the bowl.

In a large, deep pot, heat oil and sauté onions until limp. Add chiles, tomatoes, oregano, garlic powder, salt, and cumin. Add water. Bring to a steady boil. Meanwhile, in a large bowl, combine ground beef, eggs, flour, salt, pepper, and garlic powder. Wet your hands and form mixture into 1-inch meatballs. Drop them into the boiling soup one by one. Simmer 45 minutes.

MAKES 8 SERVINGS.   *Traditional*

2	tablespoons vegetable oil
2	bunches green onions, chopped
1	(7-ounce) can chopped green chiles, or 2 (4-ounce) cans chopped green chiles, or 8 green chiles, roasted, peeled, and chopped
1	(28-ounce) can diced tomatoes, with juice
1	tablespoon dried oregano
1	teaspoon garlic powder
1	teaspoon salt
1	teaspoon ground cumin
1	quart water

For meatballs:

2	pounds very lean ground beef
2	eggs
½	cup flour
½	teaspoon salt
½	teaspoon black pepper
½	teaspoon garlic powder

Grilled Chicken Corn Chowder

2	tablespoons oil, or nonstick cooking spray
2	large stalks celery, finely chopped
1	large onion, finely chopped
2	tablespoons flour
1	teaspoon salt
½	teaspoon pepper
4	small potatoes, diced
1	(32-ounce) can chicken broth
1	(15-ounce) can whole-kernel corn, with liquid
1	(15-ounce) can cream-style corn
2	large boneless, skinless chicken breasts, grilled and cut into 1-inch cubes
½	red bell pepper, diced
1	cup skim milk

The traditional corn chowder didn't seem to be a complete meal in a bowl until we threw in some grilled chicken. Wow! You'll love it. You'll want to make a couple of extra chicken breasts the next time you're at the grill, so you can freeze them for this soup.

Heat oil in a large, deep pot or coat generously with nonstick cooking spray. Sauté the celery and onion for 2 to 3 minutes. Sprinkle with flour and stir vigorously to form a paste or roux. Add salt and pepper and cook for about 30 seconds. Put potatoes in a 4-cup measure and add water to make 4 cups. Add potatoes, with water, and broth to soup. Stir to blend and cook over medium heat until the potatoes are just tender, about 10 minutes. Add the corn, chicken, and red bell pepper. Cook 5 minutes. Add the milk; stir.

MAKES 10 SERVINGS.

Second Time Around

Slightly Southwestern Fish Soup

An excellent, fast way to use any kind of whitefish that you find on sale.

In a large, deep pot, sauté onion in oil until translucent. Add garlic and cook 3 to 4 minutes more. Stir in oregano and tomatoes and cook over low heat until the tomatoes begin to liquefy; add broth, water, carrots, and bay leaf. Cover and simmer 20 minutes. Carefully add fish pieces and simmer 15 minutes more, or until fish is flaky. Do not stir. Remove bay leaf and serve with garnish, if desired.

Reheat leftovers gently.

MAKES 6 SERVINGS.

1	onion, minced
2	tablespoons vegetable oil
4	cloves garlic, sliced
½	teaspoon dried oregano
4	large tomatoes, seeded and chopped, or 2 (14 ½-ounce) cans chopped tomatoes, undrained
6	cups chicken broth
2	cups water
2	cups thinly sliced carrots
1	bay leaf
2	pounds catfish or other whitefish, carefully deboned and cut into large pieces

Optional garnishes:

Chopped cilantro, lemon or lime wedges

Garlicky Mango Soup

2 tablespoons butter, margarine, or oil, or a generous coating of nonstick cooking spray

1 medium onion, chopped

2 cloves garlic, minced

4 cups vegetable broth

4 cups chicken broth

2 (15-ounce) cans black beans, drained and gently rinsed

2 (14½-ounce) cans whole-kernel corn, drained

1 tablespoon chili powder

1 teaspoon dried oregano

1 cup sun-dried tomatoes

2 cups boiling water

2 whole green chiles, roasted, peeled, and chopped or 1 (4-ounce) can chopped green chiles

3–6 mangoes, peeled and sliced

4 teaspoons sugar

Freshly ground pepper

Salt to taste

This is our simplified version of a prize-winning bean soup from Vegetarian Times *magazine. (If you use all vegetable broth instead of chicken broth, it is suitable for vegetarians.) To save time, use sliced mangoes packaged in a jar. You'll love the sweet-sour flavors of this soup.*

Heat butter in a large, deep pot over medium heat. Sauté onion for about 5 minutes. Add garlic and cook about half a minute. Add broth, beans, corn, chili powder, and oregano. Bring to a boil, reduce heat, and simmer 30 minutes.

Meanwhile, in a bowl, pour boiling water over the sun-dried tomatoes and let sit 15 minutes. Drain and cut tomatoes into strips with a knife or cooking shears. Add to soup with green chiles. Simmer 10 to 15 minutes.

Preheat broiler. Coat a cookie sheet with nonstick spray and arrange mango slices in rows. Sprinkle with sugar and freshly ground pepper and broil for 3 to 5 minutes. Cut into chunks and add to soup with salt and pepper to taste.

MAKES 8 SERVINGS. **Quick and Easy**

Beef (Cocida) Soup

John Throuvalas and Nick Karandreas, who are Greek, own one of our favorite Mexican food restaurants in Phoenix. We became friends and Friday-night regulars. Occasionally, John would appear from the kitchen with some special concoction. Often these creations were some of the finest soups we had ever tasted. Kim couldn't get this one off her mind and John graciously provided the recipe, which we cut down for home kitchens. You will love the rich flavors of this hearty, chunky soup.

¼	cup flour
¼	teaspoon salt
⅛	teaspoon pepper
2	pounds beef short ribs
1	tablespoon oil (or use nonstick cooking spray)
2	carrots, peeled and chopped
2	stalks celery, chopped
1	medium white onion, coarsely chopped
2	medium ripe tomatoes, coarsely chopped
16	cups water
1	teaspoon sage
1	teaspoon cumin
8	small white rose potatoes, quartered
8	ounces, (½ of a one pound package) rotelle pasta
1½	cups chopped fresh cauliflower
1½	cups chopped fresh broccoli
	Cilantro for garnish (optional)

Mix flour, salt, and pepper on a plate and coat the ribs with this mixture. Meanwhile, heat a large, deep pot over medium heat. When hot, pour in oil or generously coat with nonstick cooking spray. Add meat to the pan and brown. When brown on all sides, pile ribs on one side of the pan. Add the carrots, celery, and onion. Sauté for 3 minutes, scraping the bottom of the pan.

Add the tomatoes and stir for 5 minutes. Add the water and spices. Simmer for 25 minutes. Add the potatoes and simmer for 10 minutes. Add the pasta, cauliflower, and broccoli and cook about 10 more minutes.

Remove the ribs. Cut the meat from the bones and dice. Return the meat to the pot. Serve garnished with chopped cilantro, if desired.

MAKES 10 SERVINGS.

Desert Fish Soup

High-quality frozen fillets of fish are almost universally available these days, a nice alternative to sometimes-pricey fresh fish. Use either in this great soup, which is inspired by our annual treks to the Sea of Cortez in Puerto Peñasco, Mexico. Shrimp are farmed there, and we stock our freezers for the year.

In a large, deep pot, heat olive oil and sauté onion, carrots, and bell pepper. Add garlic and thyme. Stir and cook one minute. Add broth, sherry, and tomatoes. Simmer 10 minutes. Add fish and shrimp. Cook 10 minutes, or until done. Add parsley. Take care not to overcook the fish.

MAKES 6 SERVINGS.

1	tablespoon olive oil
1	medium onion, chopped
2	medium carrots, peeled and chopped
1	small yellow bell pepper, chopped
2	teaspoons granulated garlic
2	teaspoons dried thyme
8	cups seafood broth (see recipe on page 9) or vegetable broth or water
½	cup dry sherry
2	(14½-ounce) cans tomatoes
3	fillets (4 ounces each) of orange roughy, cubed
1	pound shrimp, peeled
2	tablespoons dried parsley, or 1 tablespoon chopped fresh parsley

Cold Cockteil de Camerones Soup

6 cups water

1 cup catsup

Juice of 6 limes (use a juicer if you have one)

½ cup salsa (see recipe on page 28, or use your favorite chunky bottled salsa)

3 tablespoons chopped cilantro

1 large cucumber, seeded and chopped

2 stalks celery, chopped (about ½ cup)

Hot sauce

1 pound cooked shrimp (cut up, if large)

1 ripe avocado, chopped (optional)

Mexican seafood cocktails, packed with vegetables, blow away the stateside versions of shrimp cocktail. Served as snacks in to-go cups or as popular lunches or appetizers, they were the inspiration for this soup, a cousin of gazpacho. Please do not be put off by the secret ingredient, catsup, which is an authentic Mexican touch! Its sweetness complements the shrimp. Judy's husband, Dave, doesn't really care for cold soups or seafood soups, but he loves this one. So will you.

In a large bowl, whisk together the water, catsup, and lime juice. Add salsa, cilantro, cucumber, celery, and hot sauce to taste. Add shrimp and avocado, if using. Cover and refrigerate until well chilled. Taste again for seasoning before serving.

MAKES 8 SERVINGS.

Christmas Posole

*The red, white, and green in this soup makes for a decorative,
delicious holiday meal. For a Christmas Eve feast, Southwestern
style, serve with tamales (the green corn variety, if you are lucky
enough to get them), corn chips, and guacamole. ¡Feliz Navidad!*

In a large, deep pot, heat the oil and add onion, garlic, and chicken,
stirring until the onions start to wilt and the chicken is just turning
white. Add green chiles and cook 1 to 2 minutes, stirring. Add
hominy, tomatoes, water, chili powder, cumin, and oregano. Bring
to a boil, lower heat, and simmer 20 to 30 minutes.

Serve with separate bowls of lime or lemon wedges, radishes,
and cilantro, so each diner may garnish his or her own bowl.

MAKES 6 SERVINGS.

1	tablespoon oil or butter
½	large onion, chopped
½	head garlic (about 5 cloves), minced
1	pound boneless, skinless chicken breast, cubed
1	(4-ounce) can whole green chiles, cut into strips, or 4 roasted, peeled, seeded green chiles cut into strips
1	(29-ounce) can white hominy
1	(14.5-ounce) can stewed tomatoes
2	cups water
1	teaspoon chili powder
½	teaspoon ground cumin
½	teaspoon dried oregano

Optional garnishes:

Lime or lemon wedges

Sliced radishes

Chopped cilantro

Lentil Lime Soup

2	cups French green lentils (the tiny ones)
11	cups water
2	teaspoons salt
1	teaspoon freshly cracked black pepper
1½	teaspoons ground cumin
2	teaspoons chopped fresh oregano
3	bay leaves
1	(4-ounce) can whole green chiles, or 4 green chiles, roasted, peeled, and seeded
¼	of a red bell pepper, finely chopped
1	large carrot, peeled, and finely chopped
	Juice of 8 limes
3	tablespoons olive oil

We love lentils for their flavor as well as convenience—they don't require presoaking. A classic cookbook for both reference and great recipes from New Mexico, Huntley Dent's The Feast of Santa Fe, *inspired this Southwestern-style lentil soup.*

In a large, deep pot, cook lentils in 8 cups of the water with salt, pepper, cumin, oregano, and bay leaves for 45 minutes. Remove 1 cup of the lentils and purée in a blender with the green chiles. Return to the pot along with the remaining 3 cups water. Return to a boil and cook for about 5 minutes. Turn off heat and add the bell pepper and carrot. Before serving, squeeze in the lime juice and add the oil.

When reheating this soup, do not boil.

MAKES 6 TO 8 SERVINGS.   *Don't Miss!*

A bowl of stew is basic peasant food, and that fascinates us. When the weather cools, our souls crave stew. And we have them here for you in all varieties, from slow-cooker stews made with just four convenient products to descendents of French peasant elegance. Many are related to the thick, one-pot meals that were made by inhabitants of this region eons ago.

We learned a lot making stews and chilis. Slow cookers are made for these recipes, for drawing out the flavors over long, gentle heat. If you have the time, browning the meat for a stew adds layers of flavor that are well worth the effort. Do it in batches and take your time, so that each cube of meat is seared. Then deglaze the pan with a favorite liquid—red wine, broth, consommé, water—and scrape at those crusty bits where the flavor is stored.

Another aspect of stew and chili that we love is that they are better when made a day ahead and reheated. So go ahead: Make a stew, make a chili, make a memory for your family or friends. Talk about comfort food—tell your pals you're making stew and they're invited. You'll be surprised how well they respond. And you can enjoy their company while the meal cooks itself.

Midwestern Chili

1	tablespoon oil
1	onion, chopped
2	stalks celery, halved lengthwise and sliced
4	cloves garlic, sliced (or minced if you prefer)
1	pound lean ground beef
1	(29-ounce) can tomato sauce
1	(14½-ounce) can ready-cut tomatoes
1	(27-ounce) can dark red kidney beans
1½	cups water

Nothing beats a great bowl of chili. It is the all-American meal, but the variations on the theme are endless (check out the next chili cook-off). The claim to fame of many a chili is, of course, the heat it packs. But for the typical Northerner, heat may not be a good thing. If you're in this group, or even if you aren't, this approachable chili is for you. It makes up in about 10 minutes and may simmer for as little or as long as you like. Don't balk at the inclusion of celery—it's the secret ingredient.

Bev Walker makes a similar version of this, sans celery, in her slow cooker. She suggests serving it over a baked potato or cooked pasta.

We all like to top this with shredded cheese or a dollop of sour cream.

In a large, deep pot, heat the oil and add onion, celery, and garlic. Sauté for 2 minutes. Add ground beef. Cook, stirring, until meat is brown. Add remaining ingredients and stir to combine. Simmer for at least 20 minutes.

MAKES 6 SERVINGS.  **Quick and Easy**

Variation: Midwestern Chili for Fifty

Sarah Staley adapted this recipe to feed the hordes of people she often entertains. This one held its own at the Wilhoit, Arizona, chili cook-off, a fund raiser for their volunteer fire department.

In a very large stockpot, brown meat. Add remaining ingredients, seasoning to taste with salt and pepper, and bring to a simmer. Cook for about an hour, stirring occasionally.

MAKES 50 SERVINGS.

Entertaining

5	pounds ground beef
1	bunch celery, cleaned, trimmed, and sliced
1	large onion, diced
1	restaurant-size (#10) can red kidney beans (12 to 13 cups)
1	restaurant-size (#10) can tomato sauce (12 to 13 cups)
1	(27-ounce) can red chili sauce
	Salt and black pepper

Chicken and Noodles

The secret shortcut in this recipe is frozen egg noodles. If you like this dish, be sure to check out the Chicken Spaghetti recipe on page 109. They're both from Judy's aunt in Oklahoma, Jimmie Jamison, who made this for a family reunion potluck.

Bring broth to a rolling boil in a small stockpot. Add noodles and stir. Cook according to package directions. Five minutes before the noodles are done, add the chicken.

Serve in bowls with broth.

MAKES 6 TO 8 GENEROUS SERVINGS.

Family Favorite

6	cups chicken broth, preferably homemade or canned low-sodium
1	(12-ounce) package frozen egg noodles
	About 3 cups cooked chicken
	Salt and freshly ground black pepper to taste

Black-Bean Chili

2	(15-ounce) cans black beans
2	cups puréed tomatoes
2–3	cups chicken broth, water, or vegetable broth
1	onion, chopped
1	teaspoon minced garlic
2	teaspoons chili powder
1	teaspoon dried oregano
½	teaspoon ground cumin
½	teaspoon salt, or to taste
	Freshly ground black pepper

For garnishes:

	Real Salsa (page 28) or your favorite salsa
2	tablespoons chopped onions
½	cup shredded Cheddar cheese

This super-simple chili recipe is a cinch in a slow cooker! Great for casual entertaining. We made both this and White Chili (recipe follows) for a "Souper Bowl" party.

In a large, deep pot or slow cooker, combine beans with all ingredients except salt and pepper. Cover and simmer for 30 minutes to 1 hour, or for up to 8 hours on low heat in slow cooker. Season with salt and pepper to taste. Serve with salsa, chopped onions, and shredded cheese, if desired.

MAKES 8 TO 12 SERVINGS.

Slow Cooker

White Chili

White chili is a new classic! We suggest you make a huge batch, half to eat now and half to freeze for your next tailgate party or any informal entertaining occasion. This freezes beautifully, and the flavor improves after a couple of days in the fridge.

In a large, deep pot, heat olive oil and sauté the onion, green chiles, garlic, cumin, white pepper, oregano, cayenne, cloves, and chicken. Add chicken broth and beans. Bring to a boil, reduce heat. Simmer 2 hours if using soaked beans, or 20 minutes if using canned beans.

    Serve topped with shredded Monterey jack cheese. For parties, offer one or several garnish options: chopped cilantro, sour cream, or salsa.

    Slow cooker preparation: Sauté vegetables and chicken in a skillet. Transfer to a slow cooker and add broth and beans. Cook on low for 8 hours.

MAKES 8 SERVINGS.

1	tablespoon olive oil
1	onion, chopped
1	(4-ounce) can chopped green chiles
2	cloves garlic, minced
2	teaspoons powdered cumin
2	teaspoons white pepper
2	teaspoons oregano
¾	teaspoon cayenne pepper
¼	teaspoon ground cloves
4	boneless, skinless chicken breasts, cubed
6	cups chicken broth
1	pound Great Northern beans, soaked (see Basic Pinto Beans on page 11), or 2 (14.5-ounce) cans beans
	Monterey jack cheese, shredded

Beef Pecadillo Dip

1½   pounds lean ground beef

1   cup diced tomatoes

1   cup chopped onion

½   cup chopped red pepper

1   cup slivered, toasted almonds

1   teaspoon salt

1   teaspoon pepper

2   cloves garlic, minced

½   cup raisins

¾   cup beef broth

1   (6-ounce) can ripe olives, drained
      and chopped

6   ounces fresh mushrooms,
      chopped

1   (10-ounce) can tomatoes and
      green chiles, such as Ro-Tel
      brand

     Corn chips or tortilla chips

This is another old Mexican-Southwestern concept: A big beefy dip to eat with tortilla chips! We were inspired by a similar recipe in the Arizona Cowbelles' 60th Anniversary Cookbook, Beef Up Your Life, *published in 1999 as part of the legacy of women who supported ranching. We raise a chip in salute. And, yes, the almonds and raisins are standard. This is one of our absolute favorite recipes.*

Brown beef in a large skillet. Drain well. Add remaining ingredients (except corn chips). Cover and simmer 2 hours, stirring occasionally. Serve with corn chips.

Note: This reheats well, so you can make it ahead for parties.

MAKES 20 OR MORE APPETIZER SERVINGS.

Caldito

John Samora of Phoenix grew up in the culinary traditions of southern Colorado and northern New Mexico, and is passionate about sharing his love of those traditions. This stew, whose name translates as "little cauldron," is what his mother used to make during the fall green-chile harvest. John told us he has run into similar lamb stews on Native American reservations.

While we were producing this book, John gave us not only this recipe but also fresh-roasted Farmington green chiles, dried red chiles and chile powder, dried heirloom bolitos beans, and the rare treat of Chicos, a special stew made with hard-to-find treated and smoked Silver Queen corn. Thank you, John, for sharing this recipe—and everything else!

1	pound beef, ground or cubed
1	pound lamb, ground or cubed
¼	cup flour
2	cups water or beef broth
2	pounds new potatoes, cut in wedges or diced
2–3	large cloves garlic, crushed
2	cups roasted, peeled, seeded and chopped green chile (or more or less, depending on heat level of chiles; see note below)
	Salt and freshly ground black pepper
	Tortillas

In a large, deep pot, brown beef and lamb. Drain most of the fat. Sprinkle flour over the meat and stir to make a roux. Add water or broth, potatoes, garlic, and chile. Salt and pepper to taste. Let simmer at least 1 hour, and as long as 4 hours.

Serve with tortillas.

Note: One easy way to adjust the heat level of green chiles is to taste the fresh ones you may be using. If they're on the mild side, use more of them. If they're hotter, use fewer and add mild canned green chiles.

MAKES 6 TO 8 SERVINGS.

Dimitri's Slow-Cooker Stew

1   pound beef stew meat
1   (15-ounce) can tomatoes with
       juice
1   (15-ounce) can beef broth, or
       2 cups homemade broth (see
       page 8)
1   (16-ounce) package frozen stew
       vegetables

This is so easy—a recipe with ingredients that may already be sitting on your pantry shelves or in your freezer. You may add other ingredients, if you're so inclined, but this one is great just as is. Judy is grateful to her former colleague at The Arizona Republic, *classical music critic Dimitri Drobatschewsky, who gave her this recipe years ago during one of those "what on earth should I make for dinner" discussions. She made it the very next day, and dozens of times since.*

Combine all ingredients in a slow cooker. Cook for 6 to 8 hours on low heat.

   Variations: Add additional chopped onion, carrots, or potatoes, or add parsnips, rutabagas, or any other sturdy vegetable you happen to have on hand. Red wine is a great addition. The original recipe called for a packet of beef stew seasoning mix, which is optional.

MAKES 4 TO 6 SERVINGS.

Sue's Creamy Green-Bean and Pork Stew

Use lots of black pepper in this terrific stew. This recipe came from a great cook, Sue Messmer, whose byline is Sue Doerfler in The Arizona Republic. *This is good served over rice or noodles.*

Combine beans, onion, mushrooms, garlic, meat, soup, and pepper in a large slow cooker. Cook on low 6 to 8 hours. To thicken, if desired, stir cornstarch into cold water until smooth and stir into slow cooker mixture. Continue to cook for several minutes on high until thickened.

MAKES 4 LARGE OR 6 SMALLER SERVINGS.

1	pound fresh green beans
1	onion, chopped
6	ounces sliced fresh mushrooms
2–3	large cloves garlic, minced
1	pound pork or boneless chicken meat, cut into chunks
1	(10¾-ounce) can condensed cream of mushroom or cream of mushroom and roasted garlic soup
¼	teaspoon freshly ground black pepper
2	tablespoons cornstarch plus ¼ cup cold water (optional)

Brynn's Creamy Green-Chile Machaca

Nonstick cooking spray

1 (4-pound) beef roast

1 (1-ounce) package onion soup mix

1 large onion, quartered

½ cup water

2 (7-ounce) cans chopped green chiles

2 (10½ ounce) cans condensed cream of chicken soup

1 tablespoon cumin powder

To serve:

Flour tortillas

Shredded Cheddar cheese

Chopped tomatoes

Chopped green onions

Brynn Huffman makes this every year for her Super Bowl party. Her version of machaca, the shredded beef dish beloved of our area, has a super-easy but delicious gravy that differentiates it from most machaca versions. Brynn cooks her roast in the slow cooker overnight, then shreds it and adds the other ingredients. It's back in the slow cooker, ready to go, when the guests arrive. Brynn serves it with shredded Cheddar and flour tortillas. We like it topped with chopped tomatoes and green onions.

Coat slow cooker with nonstick cooking spray and put the beef roast in it. Add onion soup mix, onion, and water. Turn slow cooker on low and cook 8 hours.

To shred the roast, put it on a cutting board or in a large bowl. Strain pan juices into another large bowl, discarding solids in strainer. Shred meat with two forks or your fingers, putting meat into bowl with juice. When all is shredded, drain meat and return it to the slow cooker, reserving juice. (Freeze juice to use later in gravy or other soups or stews.)

To the slow cooker, add chiles, soup, and cumin, and stir well. You can serve machaca at this point, or just keep the slow cooker on low until time to serve.

Serve with tortillas, cheese, tomatoes, and onions, so diners may garnish at will.

MAKES 10 TO 15 SERVINGS.

Lamb Stew with Rosemary and White Wine

You have to make this, if only to smell the aroma from the lamb, garlic, and rosemary when you brown the meat. We made a few Southwestern adjustments to Joann Weir's original recipe.

Heat half of the olive oil over high heat in a large, deep pot. Add lamb one pound at a time and brown with the garlic, rosemary, and bay leaves. Add wine, tomatoes, and peppers. Bring to a boil. Cover, reduce heat to simmer, and cook until tender, about 1½ hours.

If using pasta, check to see how soupy mixture is. Add a little more water if needed. Then add uncooked pasta, stir, cover, and cook 15 additional minutes.

MAKES 6 TO 8 SERVINGS.

3	tablespoons olive oil
2	pounds lamb shoulder, trimmed and cubed
2	large cloves garlic, smashed
1	teaspoon rosemary
1–2	bay leaves
1	cup white wine
1	(28-ounce) can diced tomatoes, with juice
1	red bell pepper, diced
1	poblano chile, diced (optional)
¾	cup fideo or broken angel hair pasta (optional)

67

Chorizo Chowder

If you have an allergy season where you live, consider making this soup then. Kim's husband noted how good this felt on the back of his itchy throat when he had his worst allergy symptoms. Serve with lots of hot, buttered flour tortillas. And if you wish to give this a different dimension, add a can of corn.

In a large, deep pot, heat oil to medium. Add garlic and chorizo and cook for 5 minutes. Add onion and green chiles. Cook for 3 minutes. Add oregano and broth. Bring to a boil.

Add beans. Stir to incorporate the refried beans into the soup stock. Season with salt to taste.

MAKES 6 TO 8 SERVINGS.

1	teaspoon oil
3	cloves garlic, minced
1	pound chorizo (see recipe on page 23 if you want to make your own)
1	onion, chopped
2	whole green chiles, roasted, peeled, and chopped, or 1 (4-ounce) can chopped green chiles
2	teaspoons dried oregano
6	cups broth
2	(14½-ounce) cans navy beans
1	(15-ounce) can or 1½ cups refried beans
	Salt

LEFT: Chorizo Chowder.

69

Cast-Iron Pot Brown Stew

Salt and freshly ground
   black pepper

Garlic seasoning or garlic powder

¾–1 pound stew meat

Nonstick cooking spray

4   cups water

1   bay leaf

2   tablespoons Worcestershire sauce

3   beef boullion cubes, or 3
   teaspoons bouillion granules,
   dissolved in 1 cup water

5   medium potatoes, chunked
   (coarsely chopped)

6   medium carrots, chunked

2   large onions, chunked

3   ribs celery, with tops, chunked

¼   cup flour mixed with 1 cup water

Cornbread

This is the stew that Judy judges all other stews by, since it's the one her mother, Bobbie Trower, has always made. When Judy was growing up in Arkansas, one of the treats of winter was when Bobbie made this stew in a big cast-iron pot and cooked it in the family fireplace. The cast iron pot hung over the fire on a swinging arm, which her dad, Bill, installed for just this purpose. Bobbie still makes the stew in winter in Chandler, Arizona—but ashes don't fall in it anymore, she laughs. We all still love it.

Sprinkle salt, pepper, and garlic seasoning on meat. Coat the bottom of a large, deep pot with nonstick cooking spray. Place the pan over high heat. Add the meat and brown quickly, stirring often. Reduce the heat to medium-low; add water, bay leaf, Worcestershire sauce, and bouillon-water mixture. Cover and simmer until meat is tender, about 1 hour. Add vegetables and simmer gently until they are tender, about 25 minutes.

Bring to a boil. Mix flour and 1 cup water to make a smooth paste. Add to boiling stew and cook about 5 minutes or until slightly thickened. Remove bay leaf. Adjust salt and pepper seasoning.

Serve over squares of hot cornbread.

Variation: For a spicier stew, omit flour-and-water paste and add 1 (10-ounce) can spicy tomatoes with green chiles, such as Ro-Tel brand.

MAKES 8 (1-CUP) SERVINGS.

Family Favorite

Speedy Tortilla Stew

Just about all the ingredients for this recipe come from the pantry! Keep these items on hand and you will always be in a position to whip up a hearty meal on a moment's notice. Thank you to Jan Trower of Sand Springs, Oklahoma, for sharing this.

Brown the ground round in a large skillet. Add beans, tomatoes, corn, and dressing mix. Stir. Simmer over low heat 15 to 20 minutes, stirring occasionally.

Serve in bowls with a handful of crushed chips on top of each.

MAKES 4 GENEROUS SERVINGS.

Quick and Easy

½	pound lean ground round
1	(15-ounce) can ranch-style beans
1	(10-ounce) can Mexican-style tomatoes
1	(10-ounce) can stewed tomatoes with green chiles, such as Ro-tel brand
2	(11-ounce) cans Mexicorn
1	(4-ounce) envelope powdered ranch dressing mix (not the buttermilk version)
	Crushed tortilla chips (optional)

Winter Squash Stew

This was a favorite of tasters at a party we had where we served many recipes from this book. You will want to make it in the fall when you have one or two beautiful hard squashes sitting around decorating your kitchen.

To prepare squash, cut in half and remove seeds and strings by scraping with the edge of a spoon. Cut into quarters. Place in microwave and cook on high for 3-minute intervals until the squash begins to soften. Remove, cool, peel, and cut into large chunks.

Heat oil in saucepan and add onion. Sauté 2 minutes and add chiles and cook for 2 more minutes. Add remaining ingredients, season with salt and pepper, and simmer for at least 20 minutes.

MAKES 6 TO 8 SERVINGS.   *Don't Miss!*

	Winter squash (such as acorn, delicata, turban, or butternut), enough to make 6 to 7 cups, cubed
2	tablespoons oil
1	onion, chopped
2	green chiles, roasted and chopped, or 1 (4-ounce) can chopped green chiles
4	cups vegetable broth or water
2	teaspoons whole coriander seeds
½	cup pepitas (shelled pumpkin seeds), roasted and salted
	Salt and freshly ground black pepper

Hurricane Beef Stu

1   cup all-purpose flour

1   teaspoon salt

1   teaspoon black pepper

3   pounds boneless beef roast (such
         as top round or chuck), cut
         into 1-inch pieces, or stew
         meat

½   cup olive oil

5   cloves garlic (2 minced,
         3 quartered

2   cups beef or vegetable stock

1   small onion, coarsely chopped

20   baby carrots, cut into thirds

2   stalks celery, with leaves,
         chunked

2   cups dry red wine

1   dried poblano or other dried chile

½   pound mushrooms, quartered

At a food editors meeting in Orlando, Hurrican Floyd shut down restaurants and the journalists had to cook for themselves! John Long of the Cleveland Plain Dealer made an incredible boeuf bourguinon for 40 people. When we made our version of Hurrican Stew, Kim's daughter thought it was Hurrican Stuart because storms have people names. It immediately became Hurricane Stu.

Combine flour, salt, and pepper in a large plastic or paper bag. Add meat, one-third at a time, shaking to coat.

    Heat oil over medium-high heat in a large, deep pot or Dutch oven. Add half the meat and half the minced garlic. Cook, stirring occasionally and scraping the bottom of the pan, until the meat is well browned. Remove with a slotted spoon and keep warm. Add the rest of the meat and minced garlic and brown well. Return reserved beef to pan.

    Pour in 1 cup of stock, scraping the bottom of the pan to loosen any remaining scraps. Simmer until slightly thickened. Add onion, carrots, celery, the remaining 1 cup of stock, red wine, and enough water to cover. Stir well. Add chile. Heat to a simmer and cook for about 3 hours, stirring occasionally. In the last half hour, remove the chile (this is a must) and add mushrooms.

MAKES 10 SERVINGS.

Spicy Eggplant Stew for Two

This is best made a day ahead and shared with someone you love.

Combine eggplant, tomatoes, onion, bell pepper, thyme, garlic, and pepper in a medium saucepan. Heat on low. The liquid level will seem inadequate, but the eggplant will sweat. Simmer, covered, stirring occasionally, until all vegetables are tender, about an hour. Season to taste with salt.

Serve with a sprinkle of Parmesan, if desired.

MAKES 2 LARGE OR 4 SMALL SERVINGS.

1	large eggplant, peeled and cubed
1	(10-ounce) can tomatoes with green chiles, such as Ro-Tel brand
½	onion, chopped
½	red bell pepper, chopped
	Pinch of thyme
	Pinch of garlic powder
	Generous dusting of freshly ground black pepper
	Salt
	Sprinkle of grated Parmesan cheese (optional)

Oven Beef Stew

2	pounds beef stew meat
3	large celery stalks, diced
5	carrots, diced
2	parsnips, diced
2	White Rose potatoes, diced
2	medium onions, quartered
	Salt and pepper
2	tablespoons quick-cooking tapioca, such as Minute brand
1	(14½-ounce) can stewed tomatoes, diced, with liquid, or ¾ cup chopped tomatoes with juice
½	cup dry red wine
2	bay leaves
1	package beef stew seasoning mix, or 2 tablespoons Herbal Seasoning Mix, optional

This is our version of a longtime recipe favorite from The Arizona Republic *food section pages. Once you put it together, you forget about it for the afternoon. Tapioca thickens the sauce. You can use packaged beef stew seasoning for flavoring, or omit it entirely, or make our Herbal Seasoning Mix (recipe follows).*

Preheat oven to 400 degrees. In an ovenproof 3- or 4-quart casserole or a large, deep ovenproof pot, mix the beef, celery, carrots, parsnips, potatoes, and onions. Season to taste with salt and pepper. In a medium bowl, combine the tapioca, tomatoes, red wine, bay leaves, and seasoning mix, if using. Add this mixture to the meat and vegetables. Use your hands to mix well. The mixture will look dry, but it will make liquid as it cooks.

Put covered casserole in the oven and bake for 20 minutes. Lower heat to 250 degrees and cook for 4 hours without opening the door. Don't peek!

MAKES 6 TO 8 SERVINGS.  **Family Favorite**

Herbal Seasoning Mix

Combine all ingredients in a small bowl.

MAKES 2 TABLESPOONS.

1½	teaspoons paprika
1½	teaspoons garlic powder
½	teaspoon Mexican oregano, crushed
½	teaspoon dried thyme or savory, or 1 large sprig fresh thyme

---

Roundup Fuel

We know this recipe sounds weird, but think about it: Jerky was originally thrown in many a pot of boiling water! Make this stew with dried hominy, if you can find it. This is great camping food. The potatoes thicken the broth. Since so much commercial jerky is highly flavored with sodium and artificial ingredients, we cover the jerky with water to draw out some of the salt. Skip this step if you can get homemade or good-quality jerky from a butcher shop.

In a saucepan, cover jerky with water and bring to a boil. Let boil 5 minutes. Discard water. Put jerky in slow cooker. Cover with fresh water and add onion, potatoes, and hominy. Cook on low 6 to 8 hours. Before serving, taste for seasoning. Add black pepper to taste.

MAKES 6 HEARTY SERVINGS.

4	ounces best-quality beef or turkey jerky, snipped or shredded into bite-sized pieces
1	large onion, chopped
1	pound potatoes (3 large bakers), peeled and diced
2	(20-ounce) cans golden hominy with liquid
	Freshly ground black pepper

Green-Chile Posole

Dried hominy can be found in different parts of the country. Here in the Southwest, it's a staple in the markets on "the Rez," as the Native American nations are called informally by their inhabitants. It has a different texture—similar to the difference between dried beans and canned beans. Dried hominy swells as it rehydrates, and should be soaked overnight or for several hours, at least. You can substitute canned hominy if you don't have the dried version.

12	ounces dried hominy, or 2 (29-ounce) cans hominy
1½	pounds beef or pork, cubed
6–12	whole green chiles, roasted, peeled, and chopped (depending upon desired heat), or 2 (7-ounce) cans chopped green chiles
3	large cloves garlic
2	bay leaves
2	teaspoons Mexican oregano
	Salt and freshly ground black pepper

If using dried hominy, rinse and cover with water in a large, deep pot or Dutch oven. Cover and simmer on low until softened, about 2 hours.

Add all other ingredients. Add more water if needed to cover. Replace lid and simmer until meat is tender, about 2 hours. Stir occasionally, adding water as needed. Finished posole should not be very soupy.

MAKES 10 SERVINGS.

Make Ahead

Vachata's Stewed Short Ribs

4	pounds short ribs (boneless, cut into bite-size pieces, are best)
1	medium onion, chopped
1½	pounds small boiling onions (about 12), peeled and left whole
3	large cloves garlic, crushed
4	whole black peppercorns
2	bay leaves, crushed
2	tablespoons Worcestershire sauce
½	teaspoon dried marjoram leaves, crumbled
1	(10 1⁄2-ounce) can consommé or condensed beef broth
1½	pounds medium-size red potatoes (about 10), with a 1-inch strip pared around the middle
1½	pounds small carrots (about 10 to 12), peeled and left whole
	Sour Cream Horseradish Sauce (recipe follows)

Chicago transplant Linda Vachata has maintained the heartland's cooking traditions while living in the Southwest for years. She gave us this sensational recipe, which instantly became one of our family favorites. It's beautiful on the serving platter and has a simple creamy horseradish sauce to go on the side. Buy boneless short ribs when you can find them, Linda advises.

In a large, deep pot or Dutch oven, brown meat (you will not need oil). When browned, remove from pan. Add chopped and whole onions to drippings in the pan, and sauté for 10 minutes, stirring often.

Remove onions and keep them warm. Place ribs back in pan with garlic, peppercorns, bay leaves, Worcestershire sauce, marjoram, and consommé. Bring to a boil. Reduce heat to a simmer. Cover pot with a piece of waxed paper and the lid. Simmer for 1 hour.

Uncover and stir meat well. Liquid level will be low. Add, in this order, layers of potatoes, reserved onions, and carrots. Cover and cook at a simmer for 45 minutes to 1 hour, until carrots are tender but not mushy.

To serve, place ribs in the middle of a large serving platter. Arrange carrots on each long side of the platter, onions on one end of the platter, and potatoes on the other end. Serve with Sour Cream Horseradish Sauce.

MAKES 6 TO 8 SERVINGS.

Don't Miss!

Sour Cream Horseradish Sauce

1	cup sour cream
1½	teaspoon horseradish
1½	teaspoon Dijon mustard
	Fresh ground black pepper to taste

Combine all ingredients in a small bowl. Taste and adjust seasoning if necessary.

MAKES ABOUT 1 CUP.

Bean and Squash Stew

Kim scribbled this recipe on a scrap of paper during a flight from Las Vegas to Phoenix. Not only has she forgotten which airline magazine it came from, she almost forgot she had the recipe until one day when she was digging through all the papers jammed in the front of her favorite do-it-yourself cookbook. This great use of squash is one of the few non-puréed approaches to adding this delectable vegetable to your soup pot.

In a large, deep pot, bring broth to a boil. Add squash cubes, reduce heat, and simmer 5 minutes. Add remaining ingredients (except sour cream) and simmer for 10 to 15 minutes. Serve with dollops of sour cream.

MAKES 8 SERVINGS.

2	cups vegetable broth
1	cup butternut squash, seeded, peeled, and cut into cubes
1	(15-ounce) can black or kidney beans
1	cup canned (drained) corn or frozen corn
1	(14½ ounce) can chopped tomatoes
1	small onion, chopped
¼	cup tomato paste
1	teaspoon chili powder
½	teaspoon dried oregano
1	clove garlic, minced
	Sour cream for garnish

2½	tablespoons oil
2	pounds rump or chuck roast, cubed
1	large clove garlic, minced
2	medium onions, chopped
1	large green bell pepper, chopped
2	large tomatoes, chopped
1	teaspoon salt
¼	teaspoon pepper
1	teaspoon sugar
2	(10½-ounce) cans condensed beef broth
12	pitted prunes, snipped
6	ounces dried apricots, snipped
2	sweet potatoes, peeled and cubed
2	white new potatoes, peeled and cubed
2	(10-ounce) packages frozen whole-kernel corn
1	large pumpkin, seeded and scraped clean inside

Pumpkin-Pot Stew

Judy acquired this recipe, a traditional recipe from Argentina, from Judy Holt. It instantly overtook our old favorite Halloween meal. We put it in the oven and head out to trick or treat. Upon our return, dinner is served! Cooking in the pumpkin "pot" is not merely a trick, and eating the pumpkin flesh with the stew is a genuine treat. The ideal pumpkin "pot" for this dish has a flat bottom and will fit inside your oven.

In a large, deep pot, heat oil and sauté meat until about half browned. Add garlic, onions, and green pepper and continue to cook until meat is brown. Add remaining ingredients, except corn and pumpkin. Cover and simmer for 1 hour. Remove all but the bottom rack in the oven and preheat to 325 degrees.

Add corn and transfer mixture to pumpkin "pot," placed on a baking pan. Do not fill the pumpkin all the way to the top. Replace pumpkin lid or cover with foil. Transfer carefully to oven (this may take two people) and bake for at least 1½ hours.

Serve this stew in the pumpkin "pot," scraping the insides with a serving spoon to include some of the delicious pumpkin flesh with each serving. Take care that the shell does not collapse in the process; scrape from the top area first as you serve.

Remove any leftovers from the pumpkin shell, as it will leak later.

MAKES 8 TO 10 SERVINGS.

Family Favorite

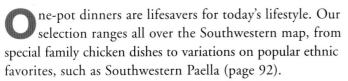

SKILLET SUPPERS

One-pot dinners are lifesavers for today's lifestyle. Our selection ranges all over the Southwestern map, from special family chicken dishes to variations on popular ethnic favorites, such as Southwestern Paella (page 92).

Our byword is convenience. Although we favor stove-top skillet cooking, some of our favorites are oven-baked in a skillet or casserole dish. We also employ our time-saving appliances because they really do help get dinner on the table! A couple of these dishes are made in our slow cooker, served for one meal, then turned into a second dinner with a little creative thought and a couple of additions. We especially love the pressure cooker, which has made a comeback. We suggest you get to know yours, if you have one.

Our kids really like the easy skillet versions of long-baked classics, such as Skillet Tamale Pie (page 106), Easy Chicken Pot Pie (page 105), and Pastor Pie (page 102), our take on Shepherd's Pie. We think you and your family will like them as much as we do!

Southwestern Fried Rice

¾   pound stew beef, very finely
      diced

½   cup barbeque sauce (the spicier,
      the better)

2   tablespoons oil

2   eggs, lightly beaten

1   small onion, diced

½   red bell pepper, diced

3–4   cups cold, cooked white rice

1   cup fresh or frozen green beans,
      cut into ½-inch segments

      Salt and freshly ground black
      pepper

The next time you have rice, make a double batch and use half in this recipe. Although a skillet is perfectly suitable for making this dish, we prefer the wok for its evocation of east-meets-west culinary art. It's also easier to control the eggs in the bowl of the high-sided wok.

In a medium bowl, cover beef with barbeque sauce and stir to combine. Refrigerate overnight (or as long as possible; even 10 minutes is fine if you're in a hurry).

Heat the wok or skillet over medium high heat. Add oil and eggs. Cook eggs until just set, but not dry. Remove from wok. Add onion and bell pepper. Stir-fry for 2 minutes. Add beef, stir, and cook for 4 minutes. Add rice and stir-fry for 2 minutes. Fold in green beans and cooked eggs, breaking egg into pieces as you stir, until incorporated. Add salt and pepper to taste.

MAKES 6 TO 8 SERVINGS.

Second Time Around

Sloppy Josés

Did you know that sugar is the first ingredient listed on the standard sloppy joe seasoning packet? Not only is our Southwestern version a flavorful change from your traditional sloppies, but you make it more healthful by using taco seasoning mix or, if you're feeling ambitious, by making your own taco seasoning mix. Your kids (and grown-up kids) will never miss the sweetness.

In a large skillet, brown ground beef over medium-high heat with onion and green chiles. When meat is browned, carefully drain the grease from the meat. Return the meat mixture to the skillet. Add seasoning, tomato paste, and water. Mix well. Cook 10 minutes over low heat.

Serve on toasted buns.

MAKES 4 TO 6 SERVINGS.

Family Favorite

1	pound ground beef
2	tablespoons dehydrated onion or finely chopped fresh onion
4	ounces (about 2 whole) green chiles, chopped
1	tablespoon Taco Seasoning Mix (page 22), or 1 (1¼-ounce) package commercial taco seasoning mix
1	(6-ounce) can tomato paste
1¼	cups water
6	hamburger buns

Eat-Your-Veggies Chorizo Bake

4   large pattypan squash, or 1 large
        acorn squash, preferably
        yellow

1   pound beef chorizo or hot Italian
        sausage

1   small onion, chopped

2   cloves garlic, crushed

½   red bell pepper, diced

1   bunch fresh kale, cut into large
        pieces

Optional garnishes:

½   cup shredded longhorn Cheddar
        cheese, sour cream

It isn't always easy to find appealing ways to eat vegetables like squash and kale. This dish combines the two with the superb flavor of chorizo for a tasty way to get that extra nutrition. (You can also use hot Italian sausage, or make homemade chorizo from our recipe on page 23.) You can prepare the entire dish a day ahead and save the microwaving until just before you serve it.

Cut the tops out of the squash as you would for carving a pumpkin. (If using acorn squash, cut in half and remove seeds and strings.) Hollow out the squash, reserving the removed flesh. Slice the bumps off the bottom so each squash will sit flat in a dish.

In a large skillet, sauté chorizo with onion, garlic, bell pepper, and squash flesh for 10 minutes. Drain.

Lightly coat with nonstick cooking spray a microwavable dish deep enough to hold the squash. Place the squash in the dish and fill with the chorizo mixture. Replace the cut pattypan tops as lids. Surround the squash with the kale. Cover. (If making ahead, refrigerate at this point.)

Cook in microwave on high for 15 minutes. Let stand 10 minutes.

Garnish with shredded cheese or sour cream. Serve in the microwave dish, carving out chunks of squash with the filling.

MAKES 4 SERVINGS.   *Make Ahead*

OPPOSITE: Eat-Your-Veggies Chorizo Bake.

Skillet Enchiladas

Nonstick cooking spray

2–3   cups red or green chile sauce,
       warmed in microwave

12   corn tortillas, warm

2   cups shredded cheese, such as
       Cheddar, Monterey jack,
       cotija, or a combination of
       cheeses

Optional additions:

1   cup shredded, cooked chicken or
       shredded, cooked beef or
       ground beef

½   cup finely chopped onion

Let's face it. Few home cooks make enchiladas any more because it is a hassle, and very, very messy. We have a solution to that! Simply layer the ingredients in a skillet rather than rolling each enchilada individually. We found it's not really necessary to fry the corn tortillas in oil to make them pliable. Simply warm them on a dry skillet over medium heat, or use very fresh, room-temperature tortillas. Rather than dipping each tortilla in sauce, just ladle sauce under and over each layer. And why heat up the oven to bake them? Just cover and cook over medium heat until the cheese is melted. The results are delicious and attractive.

Coat a skillet with nonstick cooking spray. Coat the bottom of the skillet with a ladle full of sauce. Line with 4 tortillas. Cover with more sauce. Cover with one-third of the cheese (and half of the meat and onions, if using). Repeat the process, finishing with cheese on top. Cover the pan and cook over medium heat for 15 minutes, or until the cheese is melted.

MAKES 6 SERVINGS.

Second Time Around

Barbecued Beans and Sausage Skillet

Some of our favorite recipes have been the result of rummaging around the pantry. Here is a real winner. Use homemade barbecue sauce (such as ours on page 99) or your favorite commercial brand, or substitute ranch-style or barbecued beans for the beans and barbecue sauce.

In a skillet, heat oil over medium-high heat. Add onion, garlic, and green chiles and sauté. When onions are translucent (about 5 minutes), add sausage, beans, and barbecue sauce. Stir gently and continue to cook over medium heat until sausage plumps, about 10 minutes.

Serve in bowls with cornbread on the side.

MAKES 4 SERVINGS.    *Quick and Easy*

2	teaspoons oil
½	onion, chopped
½	teaspoon garlic powder
2	whole green chiles, roasted, peeled, and chopped, or 1 (4-ounce) can chopped green chiles
1	pound extra-lean, fully cooked, smoked turkey sausage (or your favorite type), chopped
2	(15-ounce) cans Great Northern beans (or other beans), well drained
1	cup barbecue sauce

Fiesta Risotto

Kim's husband, Doug, suggested the ingredients for this risotto. His instincts were exactly right: This was the hands-down favorite dish at a recipe-tasting lunch we conducted. It would make a nice entrée for a vegetarian meal. Risotto takes a while to make, but you can use the time in between additions of the broth to set the table, make a salad, or do other things that won't take you far from the stove. Reduce the fat by using low-fat cream cheese.

¼	cup olive oil
1	cup diced onion
½	cup diced red bell pepper
1	cup diced green bell pepper
1½	cups arborio rice
½	cup tequila or 1 cup white wine
4	cups broth (chicken or vegetable)
1	(15¼-ounce) can whole-kernel corn, drained, or 2 cups frozen or fresh corn kernels
1	(8-ounce) package cream cheese

In a large skillet, heat oil over medium-low heat. Add onion and bell peppers and gently sauté about 10 minutes, or until onions are translucent. Increase the heat to medium and push the vegetables around the edges of the pan. Add rice to the center of the pan. Toast the rice, stirring occasionally, until each grain begins to look translucent. Add tequila or wine and cook, stirring, until absorbed.

Warm the broth (in a measuring cup in the microwave, if you wish) and add ½ cup at a time to the rice, stirring to distribute evenly. Cook each addition until the broth is absorbed. Stir in the corn.

Cut the cream cheese into chunks and add to the rice mixture. Stir in until the cheese melts and evenly coats the rice. Serve immediately or transfer to a casserole dish coated with nonstick cooking spray, let cool, and refrigerate. Reheat in a 350-degree oven for 20 to 30 minutes.

MAKES 6 MAIN SERVINGS OR 10 SIDE-DISH SERVINGS

Make Ahead

OPPOSITE: Fiesta Risotto.

¼   cup olive oil

3   boneless, skinless chicken
      breasts, cut in large chunks

1   pound low-fat smoked turkey
      sausage, cut in large chunks

1   large onion, chopped

1   tablespoon chopped garlic

1   large poblano chile, chopped

1   large red bell pepper, chopped

4   cups chicken broth

1   (15-ounce) can diced tomatoes,
      with juice

2   cups uncooked Tex-Mati rice (or
      Basmati or other long-grain
      rice)

½   pound whitefish, cut in large
      chunks

½   pound large, peeled raw shrimp

6   spears asparagus, cut in large
      pieces

½   cup frozen whole kernel corn

½   cup frozen green peas

¼   cup chopped cilantro

Southwestern Paella

Get out your largest skillet for this special-occasion meal! A heavy 15-inch sauté pan will do. Cover the pan with foil if you don't have the lid. This ample recipe feeds 10 to 12 people, easily.

In a large skillet, heat olive oil over medium-high heat. Add chicken and sausage; cook until lightly browned. Remove from pan; reserve and keep warm. Add onion, garlic, and peppers and sauté over medium-high heat until onions are translucent. Add chicken broth, tomatoes, and rice. Stir well and bring to a boil. Lower heat, cover, and simmer 15 minutes. Uncover and check rice. Stir, if necessary, to discourage sticking.

When almost cooked, gently stir in fish, shrimp, and asparagus. Replace cover and cook 5 minutes over lowest heat.

Uncover and check to see if fish and shrimp are firm. If so, add corn and peas. Cover and cook 1 minute.

Uncover and sprinkle with cilantro. Serve.

MAKES 10 TO 12 SERVINGS.

Sweet-Potato Hash

This dish can be as spicy or as mild as you like, depending upon your choice of chiles. It is vibrantly colorful and is as satisfying to the eye as it is to the palate. It makes a beautiful centerpiece dish to a vegetarian meal. (It is also great for using up leftover sweet potatoes.) If using fresh sweet potatoes, simply wash them and pierce the skins with a fork in 2 or 3 places. Place in a microwave oven and cook on high 8 to 10 minutes or until soft. Remove from microwave and let cool until they can be handled. Using a knife, remove the jackets.

Coat a skillet with nonstick cooking spray. Sauté bell peppers and onion for 3 to 5 minutes, until soft. Add chile and sweet potatoes. Mash potatoes and stir to combine, cooking over medium heat until heated through.

MAKES 4 MAIN SERVINGS OR 6 SIDE-DISH SERVINGS.

Quick and Easy

Nonstick cooking spray

½ cup EACH diced red, green, and yellow bell peppers (or any color diced peppers to equal 1½ cups)

1 medium onion, diced

½ teaspoon red chile flakes, or 1 small habanero, chopped, for added heat

2 large sweet potatoes, cooked

Mushroom and Chorizo Frittata

½	pound chorizo (see page 23 if you want to make your own)
2	cups chopped fresh mushrooms
4	tablespoons chopped white or green onions
8	eggs
½	cup shredded Monterey jack or Cheddar cheese
	Salt and freshly ground black pepper
1	potato, cooked, peeled, and diced

We love the combination of mushrooms and chorizo with cheese. This frittata recipe was inspired by the flavors in one of our favorite dips from Chips, Dips, and Salsas, *the first book we coauthored for Northland Publishing.*

Cook chorizo in an ovenproof skillet or pan. When it's completely done, drain well and return to pan. Add mushrooms and onions to skillet and sauté with chorizo until they start to wilt.

Preheat oven to broil or 550 degrees.

Beat eggs with salt and pepper. Add cheese.

Add potatoes to chorizo mixture and stir well. Pour eggs over it evenly. Reduce heat to medium low. Cover and cook until bottom is set and lightly brown, about 10 minutes. Uncover frittata (top may still be a little runny) and place under broiler until top is set and lightly browned, about 4 minutes. Let pan sit a couple of minutes, then cut into wedges and serve.

MAKES 6 TO 8 SERVINGS.

Salsa Frittata

Frittatas are Italian-style egg dishes, easier than omelets to make, but just as useful as a final home for the little bits of vegetables or cheese residing in your fridge. Using this basic recipe, substitute fresh or cooked vegetables at will.

In an ovenproof skillet or pan, heat oil over medium high. When hot, add salsa or vegetables. Sauté until cooked. If using salsa, liquid should be mostly evaporated.

Beat eggs in a large bowl with salt and pepper. Add ½ cup of the shredded cheese. Pour egg mixture over salsa. Reduce heat to medium low. Cover the pan and cook until bottom is set and slightly browned, 8 to 10 minutes.

Preheat oven to broil or 550 degrees.

Uncover frittata and place under broiler briefly, until the top is lightly browned, about 2 minutes. Sprinkle on the remaining 2 tablespoons of cheese and replace cover until the cheese is melted. Cut into wedges and serve topped with chopped cilantro, if desired.

MAKES 6 SERVINGS.

Quick and Easy

1	tablespoon olive oil
2	cups salsa, slightly drained, or 2 cups salsa vegetables, such as onion, chiles, tomatoes, and garlic
8	eggs
	Salt and freshly ground black pepper
½	cup plus 2 tablespoons shredded cheese (any kind; we like Mexican asadero)
	Chopped cilantro for garnish (optional)

Green Enchilada Sauce Chicken and Mashed Potatoes

You will not believe how good this is—a marriage of green chiles, chicken, mashed potatoes, and the tang of aged cheese. Look for the crumbly Cotija cheese in the dairy case; the Cacique brand of California serves several Western states. If you can't find it, use white Cheddar or feta.

In a large skillet, heat enchilada sauce over high heat. Add green chiles and onion. Stir. Add chicken breasts. Stir to cover with sauce. Add salt and pepper to taste. Cover the skillet with a lid. Reduce heat and simmer 5 minutes. Remove the lid and, using tongs, flip the breasts in the sauce. Return the lid and continue to cook, stirring occasionally, until chicken is cooked through, about 10 minutes for breast halves, 20 to 25 minutes for breasts.

Meanwhile, prepare mashed potatoes according to package directions and keep them warm.

To serve, spoon mashed potatoes and chicken breasts on plates. Cover the potatoes and chicken with more sauce, stirring from the bottom of the pan. Sprinkle with crumbled cheese.

MAKES 3 TO 4 SERVINGS.

Family Favorite

1	(28-ounce) can green chile enchilada sauce, or 3 to 4 cups Green Chile Enchilada Sauce (page 17)
2	whole green chiles, roasted, peeled, and chopped, or 1 (4-ounce) can chopped green chiles
1	onion, chopped
3–4	boneless, skinless chicken breasts (or 6 to 8 breast halves) Salt and freshly ground black pepper
3–4	servings hot mashed potatoes (homemade, frozen, or flakes)
3–4	ounces Cotija cheese, crumbled, or other salty white cheese (such as feta)

LEFT: Green Enchilada Sauce Chicken and Mashed Potatoes.

Two-Step Barbecued Beef

1   (3-pound) beef round roast

1   cup water

1   onion, chopped into chunks

2   cloves garlic, sliced

2   dried japonés chiles or other
     small dried hot chiles

1   teaspoon salt

½   teaspoon pepper

1   cup barbecue sauce, your favorite
     brand or homemade (recipe
     follows)

     Fresh buns

No, this is not a dancing dish. We make this during swim team season so we can grab a tasty, warm sandwich as we are running out the door. The two steps involve two appliances, the pressure cooker and the slow cooker. It takes just a little time to put this together over two days. We do the Day One preparation while making dinner the night before. Then we refrigerate the prepared beef overnight in the slow cooker container. On Day Two, pull it out, plug it in, and forget about it until that evening.

If you don't have a pressure cooker, you can do the entire process in the slow cooker.

Day One: Place the roast, water, onion, garlic, chiles, salt, and pepper in a pressure cooker in the order listed. Seal and cook according to the manufacturer's instructions, about 30 minutes. Cool. Remove chiles and discard. (Alternatively: Combine all ingredients in a slow cooker and cook on low heat for 6 to 8 hours.) Remove beef, reserving the pan liquids. Shred beef into the slow cooker container. Pour the pan liquids over the shredded beef. Add barbecue sauce and stir to combine. Refrigerate.

Day Two: Remove beef from refrigerator. Assemble the slow cooker and cook on low setting all day.

Serve on fresh buns.

MAKES 6 SERVINGS.

Easy Barbecue Sauce

Combine all ingredients in a small bowl.

MAKES ABOUT 1 CUP.

¾	cup catsup
1	teaspoon Worcestershire sauce
1	teaspoon garlic powder
1	teaspoon salt
½	teaspoon pepper
2	tablespoons lemon juice
½	teaspoon thyme
	Dash powdered cloves
1	tablespoon water

Spicy Ricey Meatballs

Delicious with a green salad and tortilla chips, this Southwestern twist on a classic recipe is sure to become a family favorite.

Heat salsa and water in a large skillet over low heat, uncovered. In a large bowl, combine beef, rice, and onion, seasoning to taste with salt and pepper. Form into small meatballs and drop into simmering salsa.

Cover and cook 5 minutes. Uncover and gently turn all the meatballs. Cover and cook 10 to 15 minutes more, until rice is tender.

MAKES 4 SERVINGS.

2	cups (16 ounces) salsa, medium or mild
⅓	cup water
1	pound very lean ground beef
⅓	cup long-grain rice, uncooked
2	tablespoons finely chopped onion
	Salt and freshly ground black pepper

Pork Roast for Dinner and Carnitas

Nonstick cooking spray

2 cups carrots, chopped

1 (3-pound) pork loin roast

1 large onion, sliced

1 cup water

Salt and freshly ground black
  pepper

This is a two-for-one meal: Cook one pork roast in the slow cooker for two meals. The first is a traditional dinner; the second is a Southwestern favorite, carnitas, which are little bits of shredded pork re-roasted with lots of lime juice and garlic. Tuck bits into hot tortillas, and it's a dinner of the finest caliber.

Coat the inside of a slow cooker with nonstick cooking spray. Place carrots in the bottom of the slow cooker and the roast on top of the carrots, surrounded by the onion. Add water; season with salt and pepper to taste.

Cook 6 to 8 hours on low heat or 4 to 5 hours on high heat. For pork roast dinner, serve one-third of the roast with mashed potatoes, with the carrots and onions on the side. (Refrigerate the remaining two-thirds of the roast to use for Carnitas; recipe follows.)

To make gravy, strain the juices from the slow cooker through a fine-meshed sieve. Serve as is, or heat the juices to boiling in a small saucepan and thicken with 1 tablespoon cornstarch dissolved in ¼ cup water. Cook for 1 minute, or until thickened.

MAKES 4 SERVINGS. *Two Meals*

Carnitas

Preheat oven to broil or 550 degrees.

Place shredded pork on a baking tray. Combine lime juice and garlic. Sprinkle evenly over the shredded pork. Place under broiler for several minutes, until meat is brown and crispy and liquid is fully absorbed.

Serve with warmed corn tortillas.

MAKES 4 SERVINGS.

⅔	pork roast, cooked and shredded with two forks
⅓	cup lime juice
4	cloves garlic, finely chopped
	Corn tortillas

Pastor Pie

1	acorn squash, halved and seeded
1	tablespoon oil
1	large onion, chopped
6	cloves garlic, sliced
2	orange or yellow bell peppers, chopped
8	whole green chiles, roasted, stemmed, seeded, and chopped
1	cup sliced mushrooms
2	bay leaves
2½	teaspoons salt
1	teaspoon pepper
1½	pounds sirloin of beef, cubed
2	cups water
2	pounds potatoes, peeled and boiled until soft for mashing
2	(3-ounce) packages cream cheese
2	eggs
1	(6-ounce) package shredded Cheddar cheese

Bob Barfoot checked his English-to-Spanish dictionary and told us the Spanish word for shepherd was pastor. Of course! The pastor is the shepherd of the flock. This version of Shepherd's Pie is perfect for entertaining. After baking it for an hour, simply turn the oven off and join your guests for appetizers. An hour later you can serve dinner, and it will be the perfect temperature. The squash thickens the broth.

When Susan Mathew took this to the pastor of her church when he was ill, her orange vegetable attraction kicked in. Her innovation was to swirl together mashed white and mashed sweet potatoes on top. Beautiful!

Place squash halves in microwave, cut side up, and cook on high 8 minutes or until just soft.

Meanwhile, in a large, ovenproof skillet, heat oil and sauté onion, garlic, bell pepper, and chiles for 5 minutes. Add mushrooms, bay leaves, 1½ teaspoons salt, pepper, beef, and water. Cover and simmer 20 minutes. Scoop squash out of its shell and chop into bite-size pieces. Stir into beef mixture.

Preheat oven to 350 degrees. Place potatoes, cream cheese, and remaining 1 teaspoon salt in a large mixer bowl. Beat until fluffy. Beat in eggs. Add Cheddar and stir to blend evenly. At this point, you can transfer the beef mixture to a 9 x 11-inch baking dish or leave it in the skillet. Cover evenly with mashed potato mixture. Place in oven and bake 1 hour, until top is golden.

Variation: Reduce the mashed potato mixture by half. Cook 1 pound of sweet potatoes (pierce in several places first) in the microwave on high for about 10 minutes, or until soft. When cool, remove jackets and mash with 3 ounces cream cheese, ½ teaspoon salt, and 1 egg. Swirl on top of beef mixture with white mashed potatoes.

MAKES 8 TO 10 AMPLE SERVINGS. *Entertaining*

Easy Chicken Pot Pie

Judy's ten-year-old son exclaimed, "Boston Market doesn't make chicken pot pie this good!" upon taking his first bite. Little does he know, this is a great way to use leftover vegetables, pantry staples, or the Thanksgiving turkey that's been around for a week!

Preheat oven to 450 degrees.

In a large, ovenproof skillet, combine broth, vegetables, and garlic powder. Turn heat to high. Add cornstarch mixture and bring to a boil for 1 minute. Lower heat and add chicken.

As the mixture is returning to a boil, combine baking mix, milk, and parsley in a large bowl and stir well to form a soft dough.

Grease your freshly washed hands (nonstick cooking spray is quite effective) and form thin biscuit patties from the dough, about 2 ½ inches across and ½ inch thick. Place each biscuit as you finish it atop the chicken mixture in the skillet.

Carefully transfer the skillet to the oven and bake 7 to 10 minutes, until the biscuits are well browned.

MAKES 4 TO 6 SERVINGS.

Family Favorite

4	cups homemade chicken broth, or 2 (14½-ounce) cans low-sodium broth
2½	cups chopped vegetables, fresh, frozen, or cooked (such as onions, celery, green chiles, carrots, bell pepper)
¼	teaspoon garlic powder
2	tablespoons cornstarch, dissolved in 1⁄2 cup cold water
1½–2	cups cooked and shredded or cubed chicken or turkey
2	cups reduced fat buttermilk baking mix (such as Bisquick)
⅔	cup skim milk
1	teaspoon dried parsley

1	pound ground beef
½	cup diced bell pepper
½	cup diced onion
½	cup diced carrot
3	cloves garlic, chopped
½	teaspoon salt
¼	teaspoon freshly ground black pepper
1	teaspoon commercial chili powder
1	(15¼-ounce) can whole-kernel corn, drained
1	(10¾-ounce) can condensed tomato soup
1	(14½-ounce) can ready-cut tomatoes, drained

Crust:

1	cup cornmeal
2	tablespoons flour
¼	teaspoon salt
1½	teaspoons baking powder
1	egg, beaten
½	cup milk (skim or low fat is fine)
2	tablespoons oil
1	whole green chile, chopped

Skillet Tamale Pie

The only thing tamale pie has in common with tamales is a corn-based crust. Cornmeal is used for this pie's crust, and is different from the masa used in tamales. The tamale pie trend of late seems to be beans, making it vegetarian. Just substitute about 3 cups of mashed beans, such as kidney, pinto, or anasazi beans, for the beef. Or be adventurous and mix ½ pound of meat with 1½ cups of beans. This "pie" is not baked—it is simmered under cover. And the crust is on the top, not the bottom.

In your largest skillet, sauté beef, bell pepper, onion, carrot, garlic, salt, and pepper until the meat is brown. Add the chili powder and corn; stir to combine. Add the tomato soup and tomatoes; stir to combine. Simmer over medium heat while you make the crust, about 10 minutes. (If the skillet is more than three-quarters full, remove enough from the pan to reach that level. This will prevent the vegetables from simmering over after the crust is added.)

In a small bowl, combine cornmeal, flour, salt, and baking powder, stirring to combine. In a measuring cup, beat the egg and add milk and oil. Add to dry mixture and mix. Add green chile and stir to distribute it evenly through the dough.

Drop the dough by large spoonfuls onto the top of the simmering meat mixture and spread to cover evenly. Turn heat to a low simmer and cover. Cook for 30 minutes or until the dough is slightly raised and brown around the edges.

MAKES 8 SERVINGS.   **Family Favorite**

Meal in a Bowl

This taste treat is a meal in itself and is served in large soup bowls. Upon the urging of her neighbor to "write this one down before you forget what you did," Kim's mother, Jacquie Weedon, accomplished the rare feat of capturing one of her creations on paper. We're glad she did! You will be, too.

Cook bacon in a large skillet, and just before it reaches the brown, crispy stage, add garlic and onion. When bacon has browned, remove the mixture from the skillet with a slotted spoon and set aside.

Add to the skillet the bell peppers, zucchini, and tomatoes. Sauté for 2 to 3 minutes and add oregano. Season to taste with hot chili oil, salt, and pepper. Remove sautéed vegetables from skillet with slotted spoon and combine with the pasta, beans, and cheese cubes, using the pan in which the pasta was cooked. Divide the mixture between 6 large soup bowls. Top with bacon mixture. Serve.

MAKES 6 SERVINGS.  *Family Favorite*

½	pound bacon, diced
5	cloves garlic, chopped
1	small onion, chopped
½	cup coarsely chopped red bell pepper
½	cup coarsely chopped green bell pepper
1	medium or large zucchini, sliced
4	slightly soft, fresh tomatoes, chopped
2	tablespoons fresh oregano
	Hot chili oil
	Salt and freshly ground black pepper
1	(1-pound) package spiral pasta, such as rotelle, cooked
1	(14½-ounce) can cannellini beans, drained, not rinsed
1	pound white cheese, cubed

Bacon Spaghetti

1	pound bacon, diced
1	onion, diced
1	clove garlic, minced
3	tablespoons commercial red chili powder
1	(12-ounce) can tomato paste
1	pound large elbow macaroni, cooked

Don't ask why this dish is called spaghetti, since the pasta is elbow macaroni. It's just one of those family things. Another odd family thing about this one is that several people enjoy a slice of bread spread with peanut butter as an accompaniment. Use your own judgment on that one.

In a skillet, cook bacon until about half done, stirring often. Carefully drain the grease from the bacon and return the bacon to the skillet. (You may omit this step if you wish). Add onion and garlic to the skillet and continue cooking until the onion is translucent. Remove from heat. Sprinkle with chili powder and stir in tomato paste until thoroughly blended. Combine with macaroni.

MAKES 6 SERVINGS.    *Family Favorite*

Chicken Spaghetti

This is Judy's aunt's family favorite. She doubles this recipe for her large gang and makes it ahead of time. This dish is also excellent the next day—if you have any left, and that's a big if. Jimmie Jamison of Coweta, Oklahoma, got it from her aunt, Marie Hodges.

In a large, deep pot, cook spaghetti according to package directions. While the pasta water is coming to a boil, heat oil in a large skillet. Sauté onion, celery, and bell pepper until wilted. Lower heat and add tomatoes and soup. Stir well. Gently stir in mushrooms, olives, garlic powder, chicken, and cheese. Cover and let cheese melt.

Drain spaghetti and return to pot. Add chicken sauce and stir until well combined.

Variation: To make ahead, complete the recipe and turn pasta into a large casserole dish coated with nonstick cooking spray. Cover and refrigerate. Reheat for 20 minutes in a preheated oven at 350 degrees. If you wish, top the pasta with additional cheese before reheating.

MAKES 8 TO 10 SERVINGS.

Make Ahead

1	(12-ounce) package spaghetti
1–2	tablespoons oil
1	onion, chopped
1	cup chopped celery
¾	cup chopped bell pepper
1	(10-ounce) can stewed tomatoes with green chiles, such as Ro-Tel
1	(10¾-ounce) can condensed cream of chicken soup
1	(4-ounce) can sliced mushrooms, drained
1	(2¼-ounce) can sliced black olives
½	teaspoon garlic powder
3–4	cups cooked, shredded chicken
16	ounces pasteurized, processed cheese, such as Velveeta, cubed

Easy Tuna Linguine Primavera

8   ounces linguine (if you wish, use
     flavored pasta such as basil-
     garlic)
4   cups chopped carrots, broccoli,
     and cauliflower or frozen
     mixed vegetables
1   (12-ounce) can white tuna packed
     in spring water, drained and
     flaked
¾   cup mayonnaise
⅓   cup milk
½   teaspoon garlic powder
½   teaspoon dried basil
¼   teaspoon dried red pepper flakes
     Salt and freshly ground black
     pepper

Peg Prendergast of Tempe, Arizona, shared this recipe, which has a delightful twist you can adapt to other recipes. The vegetables cook with the pasta.

Cook pasta according to package directions. Add vegetables during the last 4 minutes of cooking time. Drain and return to pot. Add remaining ingredients, seasoning to taste with salt and pepper, and toss to coat.

MAKES 4 TO 6 SERVINGS.

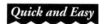

Instant Fiesta Tuna Casserole

Although we have a general aversion to those cheesy, drippy nachos commonly found in ballparks, we could not help using Fiesta Nacho Cheese soup as the base for this twist on classic tuna noodle casserole. This makes up in a matter of minutes—it takes longer to boil the water than to make the entire dish.

Prepare noodles according to package directions. Meanwhile, in a microwavable bowl, combine soup, tuna, and milk and cook on high 2 minutes. Drain noodles and return to pan. Pour in soup mixture and toss. Sprinkle with cheese, cover the pan and place it back on the burner where you cooked the noodles (with the heat turned off). Let sit 10 minutes.

MAKES 4 SERVINGS.   Quick and Easy

1   (12-ounce) package wide egg
     noodles, cooked according to
     package directions
1   (11-ounce) can condensed Fiesta
     Nacho Cheese soup
1   (6-ounce) can white tuna in
     water, drained
½   cup milk
2   tablespoons shredded Cheddar
     cheese

Green-Chile Noodles

2 cups Green-Chile con Carne,
   warmed (recipe on page 15)

1 (1-pound) package wide egg
   noodles, cooked al dente

1 cup shredded Cheddar and
   Monterey jack cheeses,
   combined

Several corn tortilla chips,
   crushed

Michelle Anderson is known for being a noodle lover. Imagine her delight when she discovered a version of this dish on the menu at a Phoenix restaurant. Her find inspired our use of this sauce in a no-fuss noodle casserole.

Preheat oven to 350 degrees.

Toss green chile with egg noodles. Place in an ovenproof casserole dish coated with nonstick cooking spray. Top with cheeses and a single layer of crushed corn chips. Bake for 20 minutes. Serve immediately.

MAKES 4 TO 6 SERVINGS.

Quick and Easy

Campfire Hash

Got leftover meat or turkey or chicken? Combine it with convenient frozen hash browns, a little onion, a little green chile, and you've got an instant, delicious meal. The secret to any hash? Letting the potatoes and meat get crusty-brown on the bottom of the pan.

2	tablespoons oil
½	onion, chopped
2	whole green chiles, roasted, peeled, and chopped or 1 (4-ounce) can chopped green chiles
2	cups shredded, frozen hash-brown potatoes or cubed cooked potatoes
2	cups diced roast beef (or other leftover cooked meat)
	Salt and freshly ground black pepper

In a large skillet, heat oil over medium-high heat. Add onion and chiles and sauté about 5 minutes, until onion is almost transparent. Add potatoes and cook, stirring and scraping the bottom of the pan often, until potatoes are nearly cooked (potatoes will tend to stick). Add meat and continue to cook until heated through. Season with salt and pepper to taste.

Serve as is, wrap in warm flour tortillas for burritos, or top with fried or poached eggs.

Variation: Add ½ bell pepper (the color of your choice), chopped, with the onions and chiles.

MAKES 4 SERVINGS.   **Second Time Around**

Chile Relleno Bake

Nonstick cooking spray

2 (8-ounce) cans diced green chiles

1 pound bacon, cooked, drained and crumbled

1 pound Cheddar cheese, shredded

1 ½ cups milk

½ teaspoon salt

¼ cup flour

5 eggs

Sometimes breakfast is good at supper time. Sometimes supper is good at breakfast time. This dish is good anytime. The bacon can be cooked ahead, making for easy assembly in the morning. This is great for feeding a crowd, especially if they are awakening after a really good party the night before.

Preheat oven to 350 degrees.

Coat the bottom of a large ovenproof skillet (or any large, deep baking dish) with nonstick cooking spray. Layer the skillet with one can of the green chiles, then the bacon, then half of the cheese. Add another layer of chiles and cheese. In a medium bowl, combine the milk, salt, flour, and eggs, and beat until smooth. Pour over the top. Bake for 45 to 50 minutes, until top is springy and center is set.

MAKES 6 SERVINGS.

Green-Chile Quiche

We had to try baking quiche in a cast-iron skillet. It is fabulous! The crust may even be flakier than most. Michelle Anderson was our collaborator on adapting this recipe to the skillet. You may use a ready-made pie pastry or our easy recipe on page 24.

Preheat oven to 350 degrees.

In a deep, ovenproof skillet, press the crust evenly against the bottom and sides, leaving enough dough at the top to crimp, as for a pie.

Spread the pastry with half the cheese. Layer the chiles over the cheese, opening them out flat. Layer the tomatoes (reserving two or three slices for the top) and olives, if using, on top of the chiles. Sprinkle with oregano, saving some for the top. Cover with all but ½ cup of the remaining cheese.

In a large bowl, combine eggs and milk and beat lightly. Sprinkle in the flour and beat until well combined. Add salt and pepper to taste. Pour over quiche. Top with the remaining ½ cup of cheese and decorate with reserved tomato slices and a sprinkle of oregano. Bake 1 hour, until top is set.

MAKES 6 TO 8 SERVINGS.

Family Favorite

1	unbaked pie pastry
3½	cups shredded longhorn Cheddar or Monterey jack cheese, or any combination
5	whole green chiles, roasted and peeled
2	medium tomatoes, sliced
1	(2¼-ounce) can sliced black olives (optional)
2	teaspoons fresh oregano, or 1 teaspoon dried
7	eggs
1½	cups nonfat milk
¼	cup flour
	Salt and freshly ground black pepper

Green-Chile Casserole

Nonstick cooking spray

5 cups Green-Chile con Carne, heated (page 15)

1 dozen fresh flour tortillas, burrito size

1 pound Cheddar or other cheese, shredded

Sour cream for topping

It is best to start this casserole with warm, rather than cold, green chile con carne. If you have made it ahead and are taking it from the refrigerator to assemble into the casserole, heat it in the microwave until it is evenly warmed, but not necessarily hot.

Preheat oven to 350 degrees.

Lightly coat the inside of a large ovenproof casserole dish with nonstick cooking spray. (We like to use a round, deep Mexican pottery bowl that is lead-free.) Line the dish with 2 or 3 flour tortillas, overlapping them as necessary. Coat with nonstick cooking spray. Sprinkle the tortillas with an even layer of shredded cheese. Cover the cheese with a layer of Green Chile con Carne. Repeat the process until the bowl is filled, finishing with a layer of tortillas covered with cheese, allowing the tortillas to overlap the edge of the dish an inch or so.

Place in the oven for 30 minutes, or until the cheese is melted and the tortilla edges are golden brown.

Serve with sour cream as topping.

Variation: Mixed Green Chile Casserole. Green Chile Casserole can be varied, just like any burrito. Adding refried beans to each of the green chile layers takes it to another dimension. Use about 3 cups of refried beans. This addition will expand the number of servings by 1 to 2 people.

MAKES 8 SERVINGS.

Green-Chile Burros in a Pan

Of all the green chile recipes we tested and made, this was one of our favorites!

Preheat oven to 350 degrees.

   Lightly coat a 9 x 12-inch baking pan with nonstick cooking spray. Place one tortilla in the bottom of the pan. Place ½ cup Green Chile con Carne on the tortilla. Fold up the sides and roll into a burro shape and place at the end of the pan. Repeat the process until the pan is full, arranging the burros in a single layer. Lightly coat the top of the burros with nonstick cooking spray. Bake 30 minutes or until the burritos are golden brown on top. Remove from oven and sprinkle with cheeses.

   To serve, spoon burros out of the pan. Top with guacamole and sour cream as desired.

MAKES 6 TO 8 SERVINGS.  *Family Favorite*

	Nonstick cooking spray
12	fresh flour tortillas, burrito size
5	cups Green-Chile con Carne (page 15)
1	cup shredded Cheddar cheese
1	cup shredded Monterey jack cheese
	Guacamole and sour cream for garnish

Basmati Rice and Chicken Skillet

¾   cup flour

1   teaspoon cayenne red pepper

1   teaspoon salt

½   teaspoon pepper

1   egg, beaten

3   boneless, skinless chicken breasts

2   tablespoons oil

1   cup diced red onion

3   green chiles, roasted and peeled,
      or 1 (4-ounce) can whole
      green chiles, coarsely
      chopped

4   cloves garlic, minced

1   cup brown basmati rice

2½ cups water

1   (10¾-ounce) can condensed
      cream of mushroom soup

You can use the simmering time during this recipe to read the newspaper, set the table, chat with your kids, or have a martini. Because all the cooking is accomplished in one pan, there is very little clean-up involved, and it's a great meal for summer because it doesn't heat up the kitchen too much. We like the toasty aroma of basmati rice simmering with the green chiles, garlic, and onion, but any brown rice will do.

Combine flour, cayenne, salt, and pepper on a plate. Place egg in shallow bowl. Dip chicken breasts in egg and then dredge in the flour mixture. Heat oil in a large skillet. Place chicken breasts in the skillet and sauté until just brown, about 3 minutes per side. Remove the chicken to a plate and keep warm.

   To the skillet add onion, green chiles, garlic, and rice. Stir and sauté for about two minutes. Add 1 ½ cups of the water, bring to a boil, reduce heat to simmer, and cover. Cook until the water is absorbed, about 20 minutes. Remove lid, stir in soup and remaining 1 cup of water until well mixed. Place sautéed chicken breasts on top of the rice. Once the pan has again reached a simmer, cover and cook until all the moisture is absorbed and the rice is tender, about another 30 minutes.

MAKES 4 TO 5 AMPLE SERVINGS.

ACKNOWLEDGMENTS

This project began in a different form more than three years before its publication. In a project of this size, lots of people are involved. We have to start by thanking everybody at Northland Publishing for encouraging our book-writing careers, and for saying "yes" so many times! You make us feel successful, and so we are. Thank you, Dave Jenney, Jennifer Andrews, Brad Melton, Stephanie Bucholz, and all the rest of the wonderful crew in Flagstaff.

We are especially grateful to the friends and family who shared cherished recipes, including Jacquie Weedon, John Throuvalas, Nick Karandreas, Jean Scott, Barbara Yost, Beverly Walker, Sue Messmer, Jimmie Jamison, Bobbie Trower, Jan Trower, Robert Trower, Sarah Staley, Linda Vachata, Mary Stutsman, John Samora, Michelle Anderson, Susan Mathew, Judy Holt, Dimitri Drobatschewsky and Peg Prendergast.

We appreciate the input and time from all who came to tastings and dinners, including Barbara Fenzl, Bob Golfen, Monty Phan, Beverly Medlyn, Susan Levy, Lynn Marino, Betty Noonan, CC Churchill, Jo Anne Izumi, Peter Van Dyke, Bob Barfoot, Helen Cavness and her sister Sarah, neighbors, etc. Thank you for sharing opinions and appetites when our families had hit the soup and stew walls!

Judy considers herself rich for the inspirational friends she has met through The Arizona Republic, including Anita Leach (plus Ben and Mark and Joseph and the rest of the crew!), Linda Helser, Diane Porter, Connie Midey, Gia Cobb, Karen Fernau, Richard Nilsen, Betty Beard, Linda Vachata, Susan Felt, Denise Namio, Kathleen Ingley, Anne Spitza, Mike Clancy, Penelope Corcoran, Alison Dingeldein, Tami Thornton, Joe Willie Smith, Gus Walker, Jaimee Rose, and dozens of others.

We will never be able to thank our families enough, for they have been behind us on every inch of the long haul. Jacquie and Walt, Bill and Bobbie and Lucile, Bev, Charlie and Vera, Mack and Melanie, Dave and Doug: We sure couldn't have done it without you.

Kim would like to thank her great-great grandmother who realized what Arizona had to offer as a lifestyle 125 years ahead of the great population shift of the end of the twentieth century. She set the generations in motion that led Kim to grow up in this a spectacularly scenic, varied, and unique part of the country. The one aspect of the great Southwest that we can share with others every day is the food that is indigenous to it.

Index

Note: italicized page numbers indicate pictures.

JUDY WALKER is the author of *Savory Southwest: Prize-Winning Recipes from the Arizona Republic* and *Simple Southwestern Cooking: Quick Recipes for Today's Busy Lifestyle,* both from Northland Publishing, as well as countless newspaper articles on food and cooking. Judy grew up in Arkansas, Oklahoma, and Texas in a big family of good cooks. She has been with *The Arizona Republic* since 1980, was named to the Arizona Culinary Hall of Fame in 1995, and is a founding member of the local chapter of Les Dames Escoffier.

KIMBERLY MacEACHERN is a lifelong Arizonan whose enthusiasm for food and cooking can be traced to both sides of her family as well as her travels. She has been practicing law since 1989, working mostly with environmental issues. She held positions with the Arizona Attorney General's Office and the Department of Environmental Quality. She is currently in private practice, serves as a Judge *pro tempore* for Maricopa County Superior Court and the Phoenix Municipal Court, and is on the faculty of the University of Phoenix. She is on the governing board of the Arizona Center for the Blind and Visually Impaired and is a volunteer reader for Sunsounds Reading Service.

The two authors live in Phoenix and each is married with one child. They are also the authors of *Chips, Dips, and Salsas* from Northland Publishing.